100 BULLETS: W I L T

100 BULLETS: WILT

Brian Azzarello Writer **Eduardo Risso** Artist

Patricia Mulvihill Colorist **Clem Robins** Letterer **Dave Johnson** Original Series Covers

100 BULLETS created by Brian Azzarello and Eduardo Risso

Karen Berger Senior VP-Executive Editor **Will Dennis** Editor-original series
Casey Seijas **Mark Doyle** Assistant Editors-original series **Scott Nybakken** Editor-collected edition
Robbin Brosterman Senior Art Director **Louis Prandi** Art Director **Paul Levitz** President & Publisher
Georg Brewer VP-Design & DC Direct Creative **Richard Bruning** Senior VP-Creative Director
Patrick Caldon Executive VP-Finance & Operations **Chris Caramalis** VP-Finance
John Cunningham VP-Marketing **Terri Cunningham** VP-Managing Editor
Amy Genkins Senior VP-Business & Legal Affairs **Alison Gill** VP-Manufacturing
David Hyde VP-Publicity **Hank Kanalz** VP-General Manager, WildStorm
Jim Lee Editorial Director-WildStorm **Gregory Noveck** Senior VP-Creative Affairs
Sue Pohja VP-Book Trade Sales **Steve Rotterdam** Senior VP-Sales & Marketing
Cheryl Rubin Senior VP-Brand Management **Alysse Soll** VP-Advertising & Custom Publishing
Jeff Trojan VP-Business Development, DC Direct **Bob Wayne** VP-Sales

Cover illustration by **Dave Johnson**.
Special thanks to **Eduardo A. Santillan Marcus** for his translating assistance.

100 BULLETS: WILT
Published by DC Comics. DC Comics, 1700 Broadway, New York, NY 10019. A Warner Bros. Entertainment Company. Second Printing. ISBN:978-1-4012-2287-1
Printed in Canada.

SUSTAINABLE FORESTRY INITIATIVE Certified Fiber Sourcing
www.sfiprogram.org
Fiber used in this product line meets the sourcing requirements of the SFI program. www.sfiprogram.org PWC-SFICOC-260

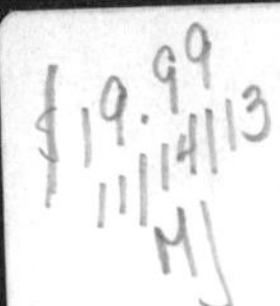

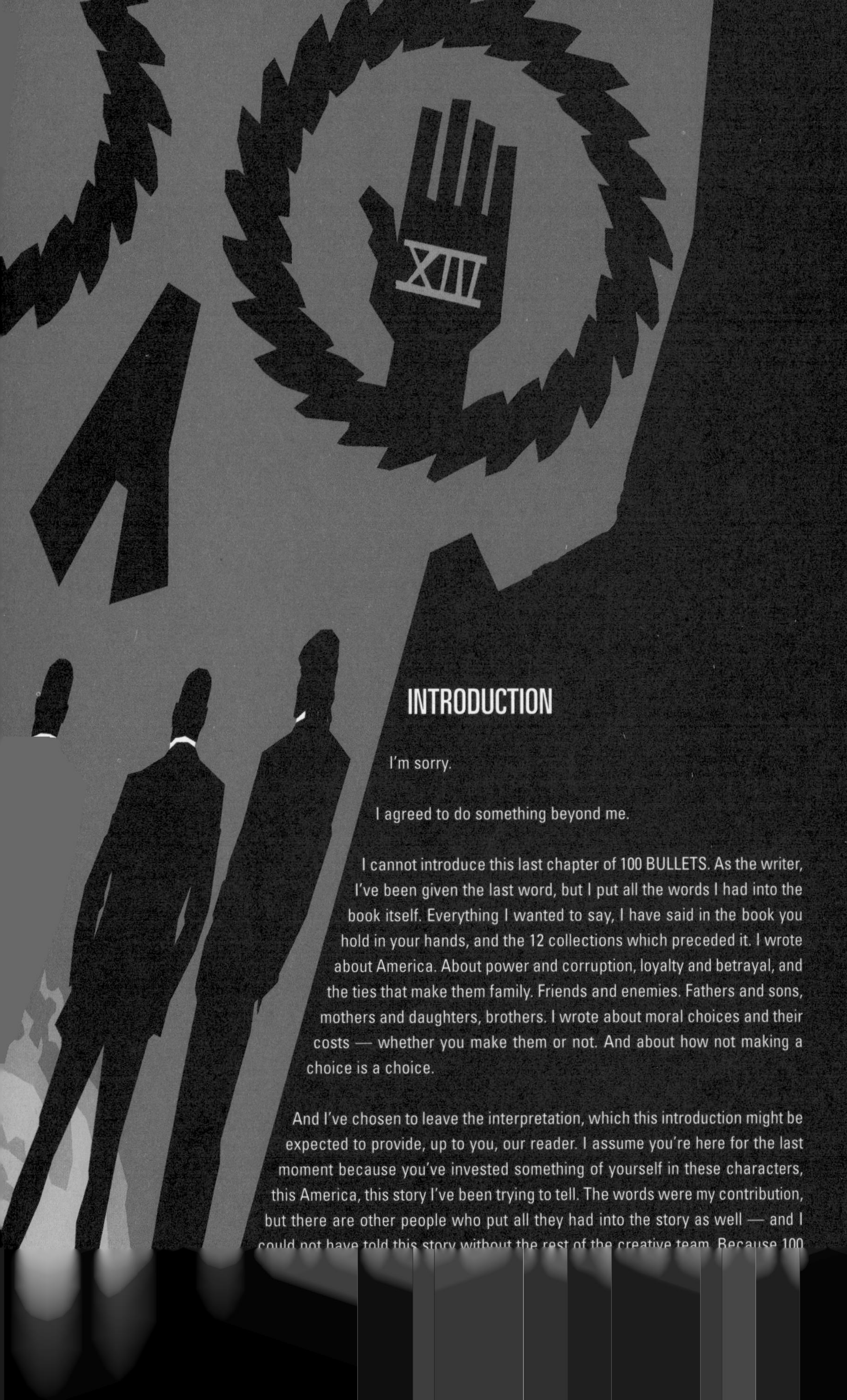

INTRODUCTION

I'm sorry.

I agreed to do something beyond me.

I cannot introduce this last chapter of 100 BULLETS. As the writer, I've been given the last word, but I put all the words I had into the book itself. Everything I wanted to say, I have said in the book you hold in your hands, and the 12 collections which preceded it. I wrote about America. About power and corruption, loyalty and betrayal, and the ties that make them family. Friends and enemies. Fathers and sons, mothers and daughters, brothers. I wrote about moral choices and their costs — whether you make them or not. And about how not making a choice is a choice.

And I've chosen to leave the interpretation, which this introduction might be expected to provide, up to you, our reader. I assume you're here for the last moment because you've invested something of yourself in these characters, this America, this story I've been trying to tell. The words were my contribution, but there are other people who put all they had into the story as well — and I could not have told this story without the rest of the creative team. Because 100

For 100 issues Dave Johnson's covers graced the book with an intensity and singularity that distinguished 100 BULLETS from every other title on the shelf. He'd take an idea, sentence, or scene, and distill it down to an unforgettable image. I mean, a pistol grip echoing the curves of a woman? Never been done before. Like Dave himself, his covers are truly original.

From the first page to the very last, Clem Robins has lettered every word written. What's really astounding is that he did it without you noticing, seamlessly blending the captions and word balloons with the art on the page. It's that skill, that sensitivity, that makes Clem's work so integral.

Color is about emotion; Patricia Mulvihill didn't just color the book, she intuited its mood. We've been in some pretty rough places throughout the series. Personally, I feel lucky to have a woman on our team, bringing a vital and unique perspective to the work we were doing.

Though the story exists in shades of grey, the real power in 100 BULLETS is rendered in stark black and white by Eduardo Risso, my partner. Because of 100 BULLETS, I'll always be mentioned with him, and that's an honor. For roughly 2,200 pages he's amazed me. He's one of the greatest graphic storytellers in the history of the medium, and it has been a privilege to tell this story with him.

On behalf of the entire creative team, I'd like to thank Axel Alonso, our original editor and architect, for bringing us together, and Karen Berger for having faith and giving 100 BULLETS a home. And most importantly Will Dennis, our editor and advocate. From the day he took over Will has had our backs through the lion's share of the series, and he shares in our achievements. He's as important to the success of 100 BULLETS as all of us...

... and all of you. Thank you, our readers, for the ride. It's almost over.

I'm sorry.

— Brian Azzarello
April 2009

100 BULLETS: W I L T

Sands
A PLACE IN THE SUN
13
JOHNSON

Sands

...NOT WHAT YOUR COUNTRY CAN DO FOR YOU--

--ASK WHAT YOU CAN DO FOR YOUR COUNTRY.
GODDAMN, THAT'S GOOD...

WE HAVE A HAND IN WRITING IT?

MR. MEDICI...

THERE'S A CALL FOR YOU, SIR.
BEANS
TUESDAY, JANUARY 21 1961

GLUG
GLUG

JAVIER?
WHAT DO YOU *WANT?*

I'D LIKE TO KNOW WHAT'S *BOTHERING* YOU.
NOTHING. EVERY-THING.

NOTHING? EVERYTHING?
THAT COVERS ALL THE BASES...

IT *DOES,* DOESN'T IT?

I MADE A *MISTAKE...*

RIING

RIING
YOU WANT ME TO--
RIING
--GO TO BED.
RIING
RIING
HELLO?
JAVIER? IT'S AUGUSTUS.
I'VE POPPED A BOTTLE OF DOM--YOU SHOULD DO THE SAME...

POW
JESUS!

NOT RIGHT NEXT TO THE PHONE, OKAY?

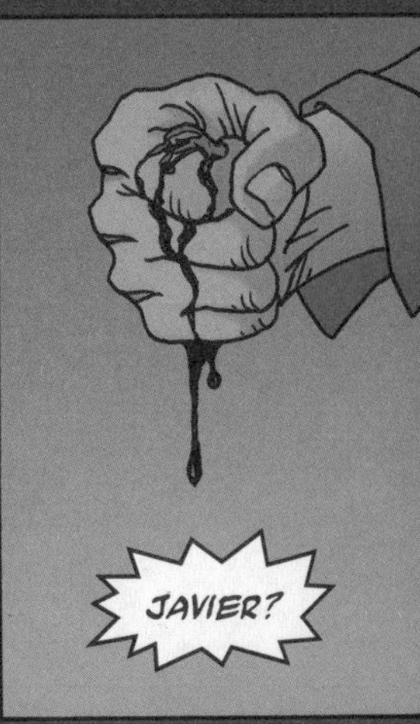
JAVIER?

JAVIER?

I'M HERE.

GREAT. I PROPOSE A TOAST--YOUR FATHER IS DEAD...

"...WELCOME TO THE *CLUB*."

I DON'T KNOW WHAT TO *MAKE* OF THIS...
WHAT THIS?

THIS *YOU*, AGENT GRAVES.

I'M IN A GOOD MOOD...
IS THAT A CRIME?
NO, IT'S JUST NOT LIKE YOU.
AH-- WELL, THAT'S WHERE YOU'RE WRONG...
GENERALLY SPEAKING, I'M ALWAYS IN A GOOD MOOD.
...RIGHT.
I'M NOT SHITTING YOU...I'M A HAPPY PERSON...
HEY, BOSS...
VICTOR.
WHAT ARE WE DRINKING TO?
HOW ABOUT...

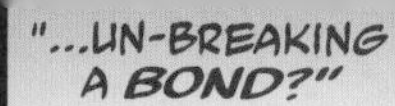
"...UN-BREAKING
A BOND?"

BD-RING
BD-RING

BD-RING BD-RING

BANG

BD-RING
BD-RING

E'YO.
YEAHYEAH YEAH, HE'S RIGHT HERE, SHOTGUN.
NAH, JUS', Y'KNOW...
KNOWS YOU WANNA MEET 'IM.
WHAT? HOW MANY TIMES I GOTTA REPEAT MYSELF, LEON?
MUTHAFUCKIN' LITTLE MAN'S A STRAIGHT-UP SOLDIER. HE'S DOWN, BRO.
YEAHYEAHYEAH, YOU'LL BE DA JUDGE.
TUMMY
WE PULLIN' UP. SCOPE YA SHORTLY.

Y'ALL READY TO MEET ***THE MAN,*** SON?

UH HUH.

UH FUCKIN' ***HUH,*** HUH?

I PUT THE WORD IN ***SERIOUS*** FER YOU. MY REP-- 'S ON THE ***LINE,*** KNOWHUM-SAYIN'?

I...

BD-RING
BD-RING
BD-RING

BD-RING

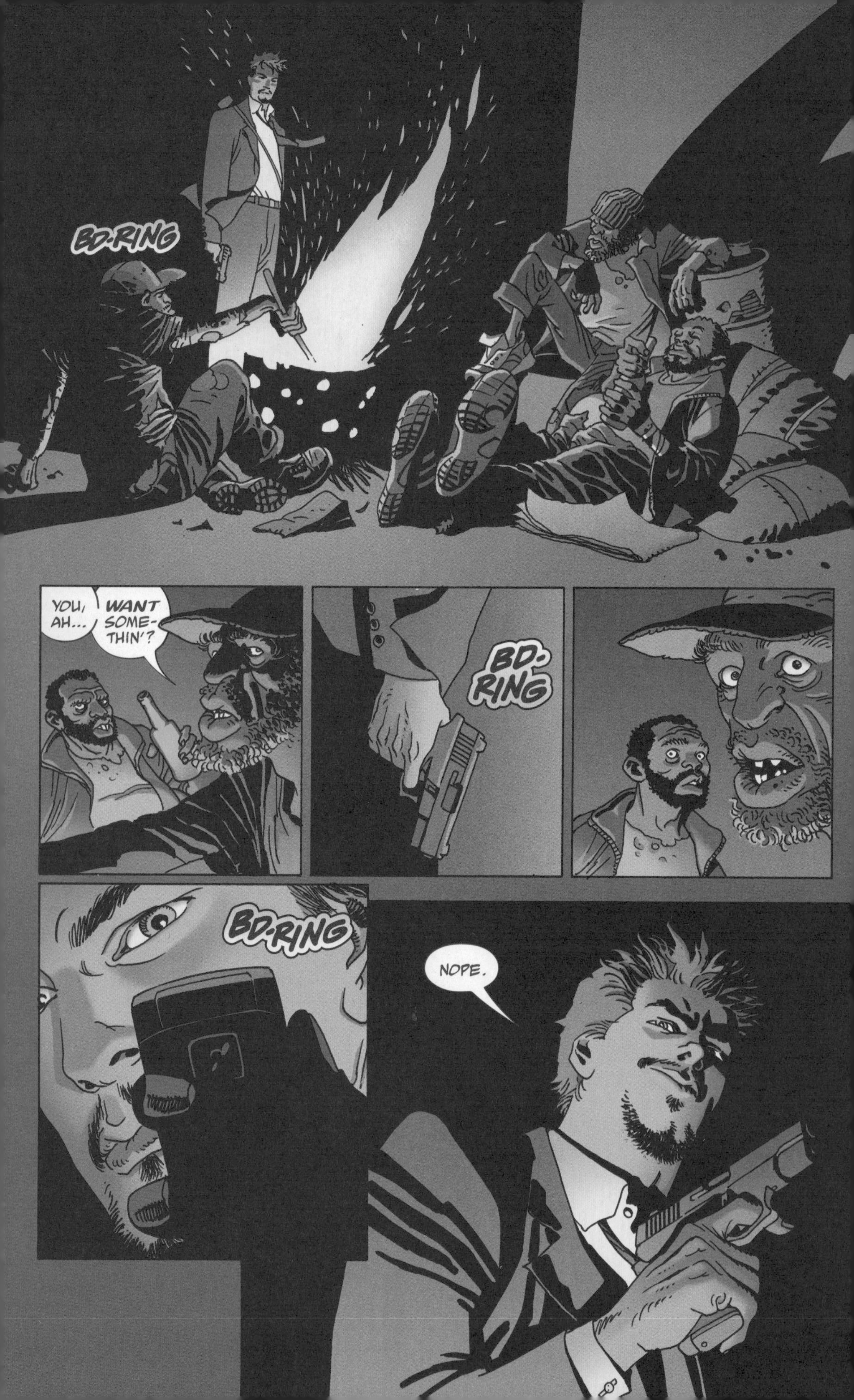

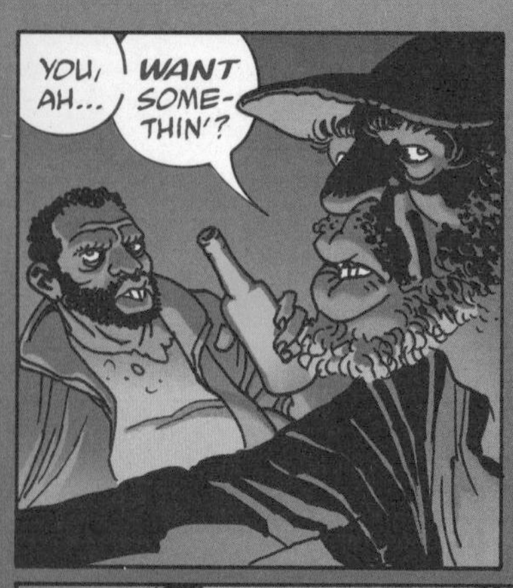

YOU, AH...
WANT SOMETHIN'?

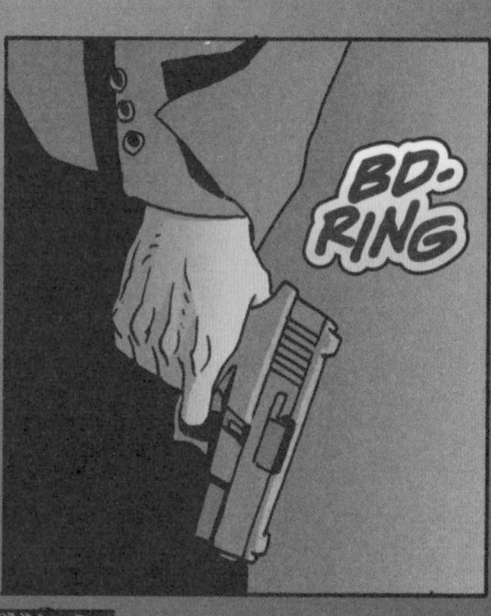

BD-RING

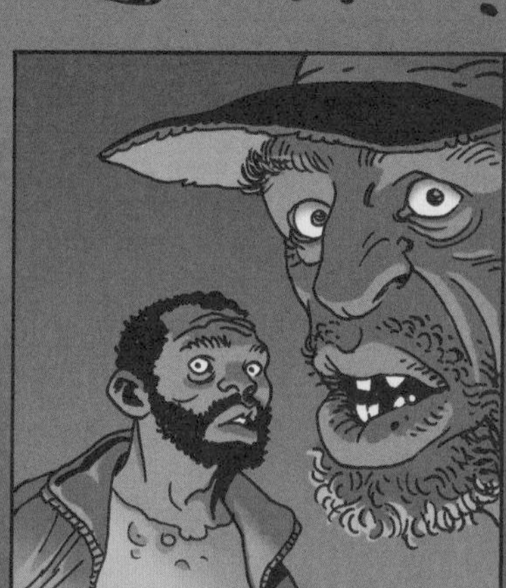

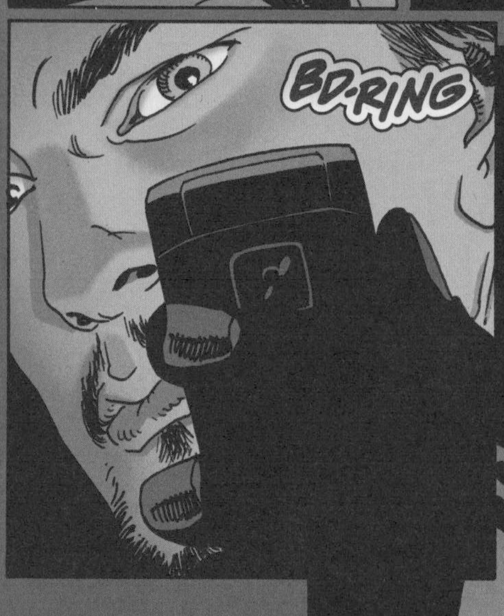

BD-RING

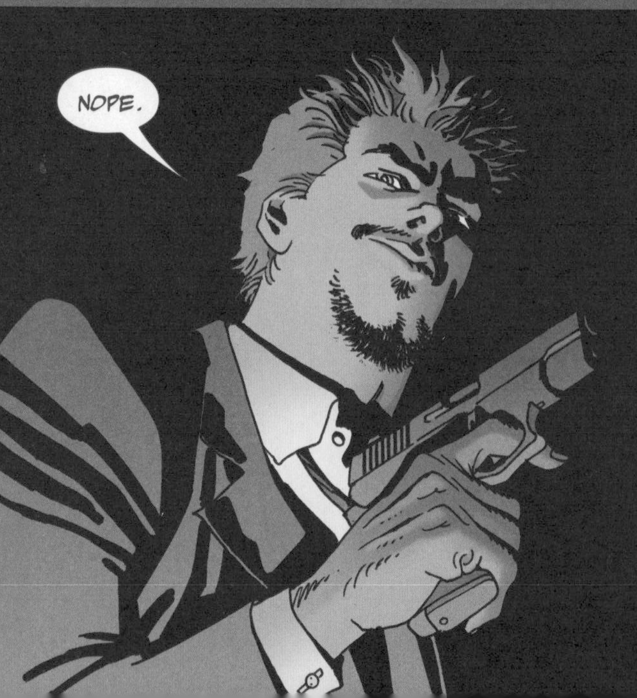

NOPE.

HMMM.
NOT A GOOD THING...
IT'S NOTHING.
CLIC
WE ARE ALMOST DONE, YOU KNOW THAT?
BAR & LOUNGE
COQ d'OR
THE LONG ROAD. THIS BUSINESS THAT WE'VE BEEN IN...
...FORCED TO BE IN--IT'S ALL ABOUT TO FALL INTO PLACE FOR US. EVERYTHING WE'VE DONE. ALL OF IT.
IT FEELS GOOD.
dOR
TO THE FALL OF THE TRUST...
...AS IT CURRENTLY STANDS.
KLINK
"LEON!"

OH SHIT--LEE, I DIN'--
'S COOL. INTRODUCE ME TO THE LIL' BROTHA.
THIS HERE'S PIP.
WHAT THE FUCK KINDA NAME IS THAT?
IS SHORT FOR PIPPIN.
HMM... LIKE AFTER SCOTTIE?
YEAH.
WAS MY MOM'S FAVORITE PLAYER.
WELL, HE WAS HELLA BALLER, BACK IN THE DAY.
BUT THE MUTHAFUCKA HAD A PUSSY IN 'IS JOCK. AIN'T GOT NO USE FER NO SHORTY PUSSY IN MINE.
CLOSE THE DOOR ON YER WAY OUT, GRAVY.

AXN
SO, PIPPEN, GRAVY TELL YOU WHY YER HERE?
HE SAYS YOU WAS INT'RESTED IN MEETIN' ME. ON ACCOUNT A HOW I HANDLE MY CORNER.
WAIT--I THOUGHT IT WAS MY CORNER.
N.W.A
IT IS.
YEAH.
JUS' SO WE KNOW.
AN' DON' THINK I DON' KNOW EVERY DAMN THING THERE IS TO KNOW ABOUT YOU, KID. 'CAUSE GODDAMN, I DO.

YER MOMMA--
GAVE YOU YER
NAME? SHE DIN'
GIVE YOU HER
AIDS, DID
SHE?
NO.
FUCKIN' NEEDLES
MAN, THAT SHIT'S LIKE...I
AIN'T GOOD. MY MOMS, SH
DIED A' THE AIDS.
SHE USED?
FUCK...SHE WHORED.
SAME DIFFERENCE,
REALLY.
YOU AN' ME, WE
GOT A LOT IN COMMON,
KNOWHUMSAYIN'?
THAT CORNER OF
OURS...THERE'S A
MUTHAFUCKA THAT'S
FITTIN' TO TAKE
IT FROM US.
HOW YOU
FEELIN' ABOUT
THAT SHIT?
WHAT--
YOU DIN'
KNOW?

SIDDOWN.
PICK IT UP.
CLOCKIN'S SHORT TIME SHIT, PIP.
I NEED TO KNOW IF YE READY FER BIG...
"SO BOSS, WHE WE'RE DONE,

...
...
AGENT GRAVES?
YES?
I JUST ASKED YOU--
I HEARD.
WE GOT A PROBLEM?
I WOULDN'T SAY THAT...
...EVEN IF WE DID.
BURNS
BD-RING
AGENT GRAVES?
?
YOU CALLED AGENT GRAVES?

IF I AM?
THEN I'M S'POSED TO TELL YOU...
...GOODBYE.
CLICK

I'M BORED, BRO.
THAT'S NOT MY PROBLEM.
AIN'T SAYIN' IT IS, JACK, JUS' SAYIN'.
THAT'S YER PROBLEM, LOOP.
HOW YOU MEAN?
YOU TALK TOO MUCH.
WHAT'S ON YER MIND SOMETIMES SHOULD STAY THERE.
BULL, SON. A MAN THAT DON' SPEAK HIS MIND GETS ALL WOUND UP ON WHAT HE SHOULDA SAID.
THAT KINDA "WHAT IF" SHIT, MAKES ONE SICK, HEAR?
'SIDES, I DIDN' JAW, I DON' THINK YOU AND I WOULD EVER HAVE TWO WORDS.
YOU KNOW WHY THAT IS?
YOU GONNA TELL ME?
I WOULD...

"100 BULLETS" CHAPTER ONE: CORNER OF THE SKY

JOHNSON

CONGRESS HOTEL

"HELLO, MA? IT'S *ME*..."

JUS' WANNA SEE HOW YOU WAS *DOIN'*.

OH, THE *SAME*. I WAS FEELIN' LONELY, REMI, SO'S I GOT A PUPPY.

ATLANTIC CITY. YOU EVER *BEEN*?

YOU DID? WELL, AIN'T *THAT* SOMETHIN'...I MEAN, I REMEMBER CRYIN' MY *EYES* OUT FER ONE WHEN I WAS A KID.

THAT WAS YOUR *BROTHER*. *YOU* WEREN'T MUCH OF A CRYER-- SPEAKIN' OF, DID I TELL YOU I GOTTA POST CARD FROM *RONNIE*?
FROM WHERE?

...I'M SORRY YER FEELIN' LONELY...
OH, I AIN'T NO *MORE*...

AM I, BAMBI?
BAMBI?
YEAH?
THAT'S HIS NAME. BAMBI...
HIS? AH JEEZ, MA--YOU ARE FUCKIN' THAT DOG--
WHAT?
NO--I DIDN' MEAN TO SAY THAT.
LOOK, WHAT I MEANT WAS IT AIN'T A GOOD NAME FER A BOY DOG...
WHY NOT? YOU REMEMBER THE MOVIE? NOW THAT YOU CRIED AT.
YOU WAS SO CUTE, I FELT SO BAD.
SO?
SO BAMBI WAS A BOY DEER. NOW HE'S A BOY DOG.
GO ON THE PAPERS, SWEET-HEART.

YOU LET HIM SH--POOP IN THE HOUSE?
HE'S A BABY, REMI.
ALL I'M DOIN' IS GETTING HIM TO DO HIS BUSINESS WHERE I WANT HIM TO.
AN' ALL I'M SAYIN' IS HE'LL GET THE BUSINESS FROM ALL THE OTHER BOY DOGS WITH A NAME LIKE THAT.
JESUS MARY AN' JOSEPH, REMI, EVERY DOG IN THE NEIGHBORHOOD'S BEEN NEUTERED. THEY AIN'T EXACTLY BOYS NO MORE.
MA-- DON'CHOO DO THAT! DON' YOU DARE CUT BAMBI'S BALLS OFF...
BUT THE DOCTOR AT THE ANIMAL HOSPITAL, SAID WHEN HE'S OLD ENOUGH--
--VERY OLD--HE'LL GET THE ASS CANCER, OKAY? BUT CHRIST, CROSS THAT BRIDGE WHEN HE'S WETTIN' YER FLOORS...
'SIDES, WHAT YOU ALWAYS TELL ME ABOUT DOCTORS?
...THEY NEVER GOT NOTHIN' GOOD TO SAY THAT'S GOOD.
EXACTLY. YOU LET BAMBI KEEP 'IS STONES, YOU HEAR ME?
PE

I HEAR YOU. WHERE ARE YOU?
CHICAGO.
OH, THAT'S CLOSE.
YEAH, I'M JUS' A COUPLE HOURS AWAY FROM CLEVO, I KNOW. SHOULD COME AN' SEE YOU.
SO WHY DON' YOU?
I'M WORKIN'. I WILL. WHEN I CAN.
WHEN YOU CAN.
I PROMISE-- LOOK, OL' LADY, DON' MAKE ME COME BACK THERE AN'--
--WHAT?
FIGHT OFF ALL THE GUYS. "YOU GET AWAY FROM MY MA, OR SO HELP ME..."
"OH PLEASE. THE ONLY GUY YOU'LL BE FIGHTIN' IS BAMBI--OFF MY LEG--I LET HIM KEEP 'IS JEWELS."
CONGRESS HOTEL
"YOU PASS THE PHONE TO HIM."
BAMBI--YOU EVEN THINK ABOUT HUMPIN' MY MA...

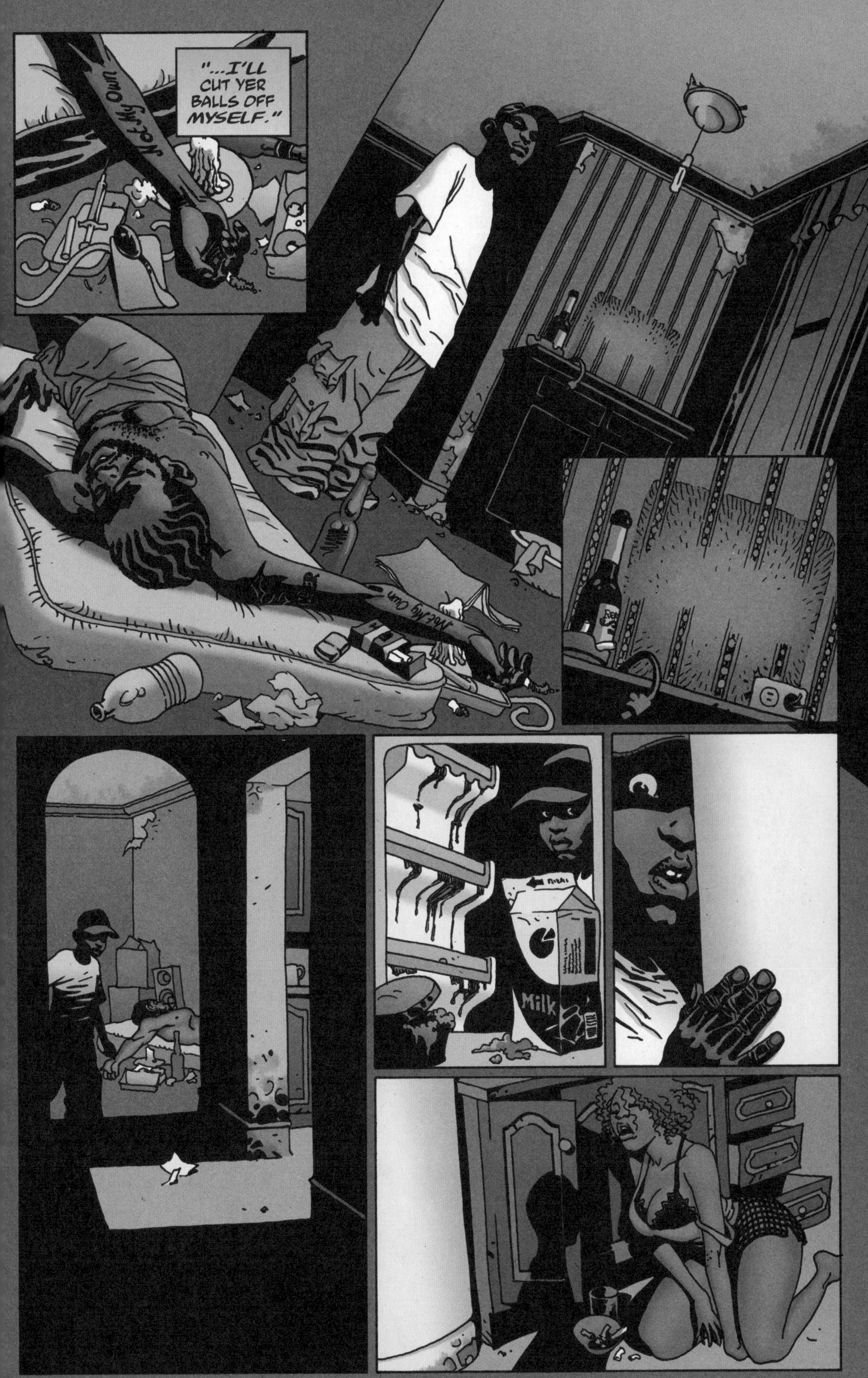
"...I'LL CUT YER BALLS OFF MYSELF."
Not My Own
Not My Own
Milk

ANDRE?
NO, IT'S ME.
OH...
PIP...
THE...?
WHERE'S THE TV, MOMMA?
...THE PAWN TICKET'S ON THE TABLE.

"THIS IS THE WAY IT IS, AN' I AIN'T ABOUT TO PUT NO CANDY-ASS SHIT ON IT, 'CAUSE YOU AN' ME, WE DOWN, NO?"
TOP GUN

RECORD CO.

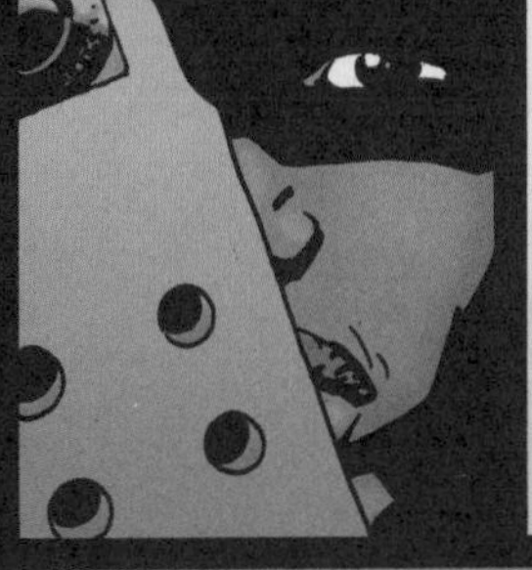

"NO, WE DOWN, LEON."

NICE ON MY EARS. SO WE GOT SOME MUTHAFUCKA LOOKIN' TO MAKE A PLAY ON WHAT BELONGS TO US.

BITCH USIN' A LITTLE RED BACK PACKIN' NIGGA TO BRING HIS SHIT INTA OUR HOUSE.
'S BOLD, SON, AIN'T RIGHT. SO WE GOTS TO MAKE IT SO.
OUR CORNER.

LEON, AIN'T NO SHIT DEALT ON MY--
--OUR CORNER, OTHER THAN WHAT ME AN' MY CREW SELLIN'! AS' GRAVY--HE KNOWS MY SHIT IS--
--STELLAR, PIP. I KNOW THAT AS WELL. AN' THAT, LITTLE BROTHA...
...IS WHY YOU ARE HERE.
I USED TO WORK THE CURB, JUS' LIKE YOU.
YOU...?
WHAT, YOU THINK I WAS BORN IN THIS? I CAME FROM SHIT...
FUCK, LITTLE MAN...THE GAME IS ALL ABOUT OPPORTUNITIES, S'ALL IT IS.
I'M HANDIN' YOU ONE. YOU DON' WAN' IT, THAS' COO-MO-DEE. BUT YOU BETTA KNOW...

"...THERE WON' BE ANOTHA."

POW.

POW.

POW.

"I'VE BEEN *THINKING...*"

"GOOD FOR **YOU**."

"I'D LIKE TO DO SOMETHING **SPECIAL** FOR MY FATHER."

"REALLY?"
"THAT SURPRISE YOU?"

"NAH, NOTHING SURPRISES ME ANYMORE. IT'S JUST, AH, Y'KNOW...

"...WHY?"

"DO I NEED A REASON?"
"NO, YOU DON'T NEED SHIT, BENITO. YER ALREADY FULL OF IT."
"YOU SHOULD BE CAREFUL, TALKING TO ME LIKE THAT."
"FUCK, SON--YOU SHOULD BE GRATEFUL SOMEONE DOES. YER RICHER THAN FUCKIN' GOD, BUT THERE'S ONE THING NEITHER OF YOU ASSHOLES CAN BUY."
"WHAT MIGHT THAT BE?"
"...HONESTY.
"LIES ARE FOR SALE. MOST COME CHEAP, AND SOME CAN COST YOU MORE THAN YOU HAVE. BUT HONESTY?"

..IS SHIT
YOU CAN'T BUY.
WOW.
Y'KNOW, LONO, SOMETIMES YOU REALLY SURPRISE ME.
LIKE ONE OF THOSE HORSES THAT CAN COUNT.
HMM. I DON'T THINK I'LL TAKE THAT AS A COMPLIMENT.
YOU DON'T TAKE ANYTHING. I'VE BOUGHT YOUR LOYALTY.
YOU THINK SO?
ABSOLUTELY.
BENITO, THERE'S A CHANCE YOU MIGHT PAY FOR THAT, TOO.
SO YOU WANT TO DO SOMETHING SPECIAL FOR YOUR FATHER. WHY DON'T YOU TELL ME WHAT, AND I'LL FIGURE OUT THE REASON.
I WANT TO HAND HIM A MINUTEMAN.

HEH. IS THAT ALL?
THAT'S ALL.
OKAY. DEAD OR ALIVE?
I HAVE A CHOICE?
SURE. I MEAN WHY NOT? LET'S MAKE IT FUN.
I'M NOT USED TO HAVING TO CHOOSE, SO...
BOTH.
FIND THEM, AND DELIVER.
ONE MORE THING, LONO-- DO ME A FAVOR. WHILE YOU'RE AT IT?
ENJOY YOURSELF.
"YOU KIDDIN'-- FER REAL?"

I AIN'T MAKIN' THIS SHIT UP, KEEN.
LEON AKSED ME--ME--TO HANDLE HIS BIZ'NIZZ.
YOU GONNA?
WHAT THE FUCK YOU THINK, GEDDY, DUMB-ASS?
44
DAMN, SON--WE GONNA BE PLAYAS!
S'RIGHT...BE ROLLIN' ALL UP IN THIS HOOD--LAYIN' THE LAW.
NO MO' A THIS CURB BULLSHIT.
HEY, PIP...
HEARD YER SIDDOWN WITH LEON WENT WELL. YOU IMPRESSED THE MAN, LITTLE BROTHA...

THAS' GOOD.
WANTS ME TO MAKE IT CRISTAL WITH YOU--HE DON' WANT THIS SHIT HANGIN'. IT'S A FUCKIN' JOB--SO DO IT...
GET IT DONE.
THE PIECE IN YO' HANDS IS ALL KINDS A' CLEAN. CAN'T BE TRACED.
...'CEPT TO YOU--SO YOU THROW IT DOWN THE SEWER AFTER. FIVE-OH'LL BE LOOKIN' FO' A NIGGER WIT' A GUN...
YOU AIN'T GOT NO GUN, YOU AIN'T THE NIGGER THEY LOOKIN' FOR, CAPISCE?
WHAT?
DON' WASTE MY ME, PIPPEN! DO YOU UNNERSTAN' WHAT I'M DROPPIN'?
YEAH. WE COO', GRAVY.
A'IGHT THEN.
CETCHA.

I'M NOT SURE ABOUT NOTHIN' NO MORE...
...TRUTH IS, I HAVEN'T BEEN FOR A WHILE.
BUT NOW I'M SURE OF IT.
WHAT'S IT LIKE, HAVIN' THAT BAT-SHIT HAWAIIAN AS A BOSS?
LONO AIN'T SO CRAZY NO MORE-- JUST MEAN. HE STILL FUCKS WITH PEOPLE, BUT HE DON' SEEM TO GET ANY JOY OUT OF IT.
NONE?
SOME. WHY YOU ASK?
YOU THINK HE'S FULL OF SHIT?
I THINK...
DINER
...FUCKIN' EVERYONE IS.

WHAT MADE YOU THROW IN WITH LONO, ANYWAY?
HE CAME AN' GOT ME...
GRAVES WANTED ME DEAD.
TALK ABOUT FULL OF SHIT.
FUCK, AND YEAH, I DO. THE OLD MAN GAVE ME A TEST. IN ONE OF HIS ATTACHÉS.
DINER
WHO WAS INSIDE?
YOU REALLY BELIEVE THAT'S WHAT GRAVES WANTED?
I WAS.
THAT'S FUCKED UP.
YOU THINK?
ZZZZZ
YEAH?
HEY, BIG BOY, WHAT'CHA WEARIN'?

UH, MY SUIT.
...
WELL GET YER WAR ON, JACK. YOU AN' LOOP ARE GOIN' TO CHICAGO.
BRONCO

"SINCE THAT BOTCHED HIT, D'ARCY HAS A FUCKIN' ARMY WATCHIN' HER BACK.
"THAT AIN'T ENOUGH.
"GRAVES IS STILL THERE-- HE HATES FUCK-UPS-- WE BOTH KNOW THAT..."
"THAT WHY YOU'RE GIVING THIS TO ME?"

"NO, JACK, IT'S 'CAUSE YOU CAN TAKE ANY ONE OF US."

"US?"

OUTTA THE SEVEN, NOBODY CALLED YOU THE MONSTER IRONICALLY, DIG?

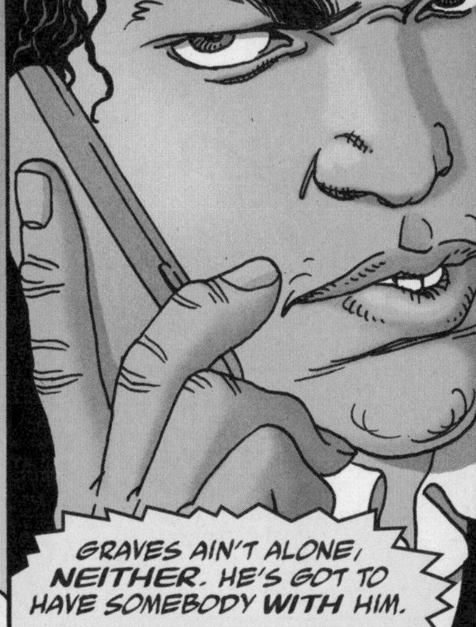
GRAVES AIN'T ALONE, NEITHER. HE'S GOT TO HAVE SOMEBODY WITH HIM.

I KNOW WHO'S NOT...

HOW'S LIFE IN THE BIG HOUSE, LONO?

JESUS... COLE?
THE LATTER. I GOT SOMETHING YOUR BOSS WANTS.
I WANT YER BOSS.

"YEAH...I KNOW. TROUBLE IS, I SEEM TO BE BETWEEN THEM AT THE MOMENT."

WE SHOULD TALK.

"ABSO-MOTHERFUCKIN'-LUTELY WE SHOULD."

"THIS IS A GOOD THING, COLE... I HOPE WE CAN WORK SOME-THING OUT."

I DON'T SEE WHY NOT.
SWEET. SAY, PUT LOOP ON FOR ME...

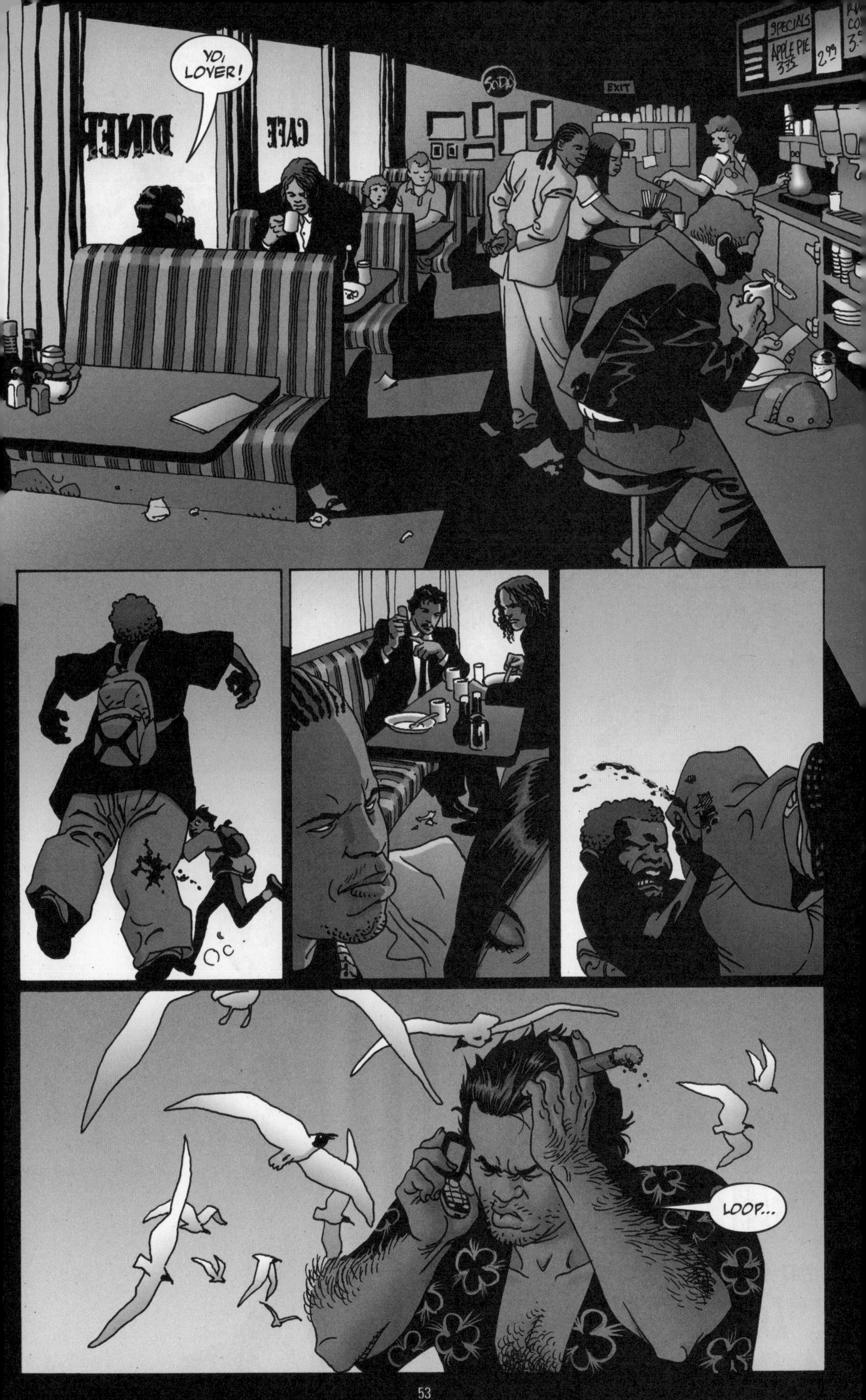

YO, LOVER!

'SUP, LONO?

LISTEN. I NEED YOU TO DO SOMETHING FOR ME RIGHT NOW. COLE, BEFORE HE DOES IT TO YOU...
PUT A BULLET IN HIS HEAD.
NOW.

"RIGHT NOW..."
"100 BULLETS"
CHAPTER TWO:
"LOST IN A ROMAN"

JOHNSON

HOFFA BOSS
JESUS, JAVIER... THESE ARE *GOOD.*
WHAT VARIETY DID YOU SAY THEY WERE?
WODKA
OLYMPIAS, AUGUSTUS. THEY'RE LOCAL.
THEY'RE SO SMALL, BUT GODDAMN, WHAT FLAVOR!
I CAN REALLY TASTE THE *COPPER.*

REALLY?
THAT'S WHAT I SAID.
YOU SHOULD DRINK VODKA WHEN YOU EAT OYSTERS. WINE OR CHAMPAGNE COMPETES WITH THE OCEAN. VODKA...
STAYS OUT OF THE WAY?
ENHANCES.
"HAH! THEN POUR SOME, PHIL."

HERE'S TO THE TRUST--THE NEW TRUST...

...AND THE MINUTEMEN.
ENHANCING.
WHAT WE'VE DONE--THE THREE OF US--WASN'T EASY. BUT WHAT WE DO...

...WE DO FOR ONLY THE BEST INTENTIONS.

MAY I?
CERTAINLY.

"TO THE OLD GUARD..."

"YES..."

"...TO THE OLD GUARD."
25CF-175
"100 BULLETS"
CHAPTER THREE: CLOSER

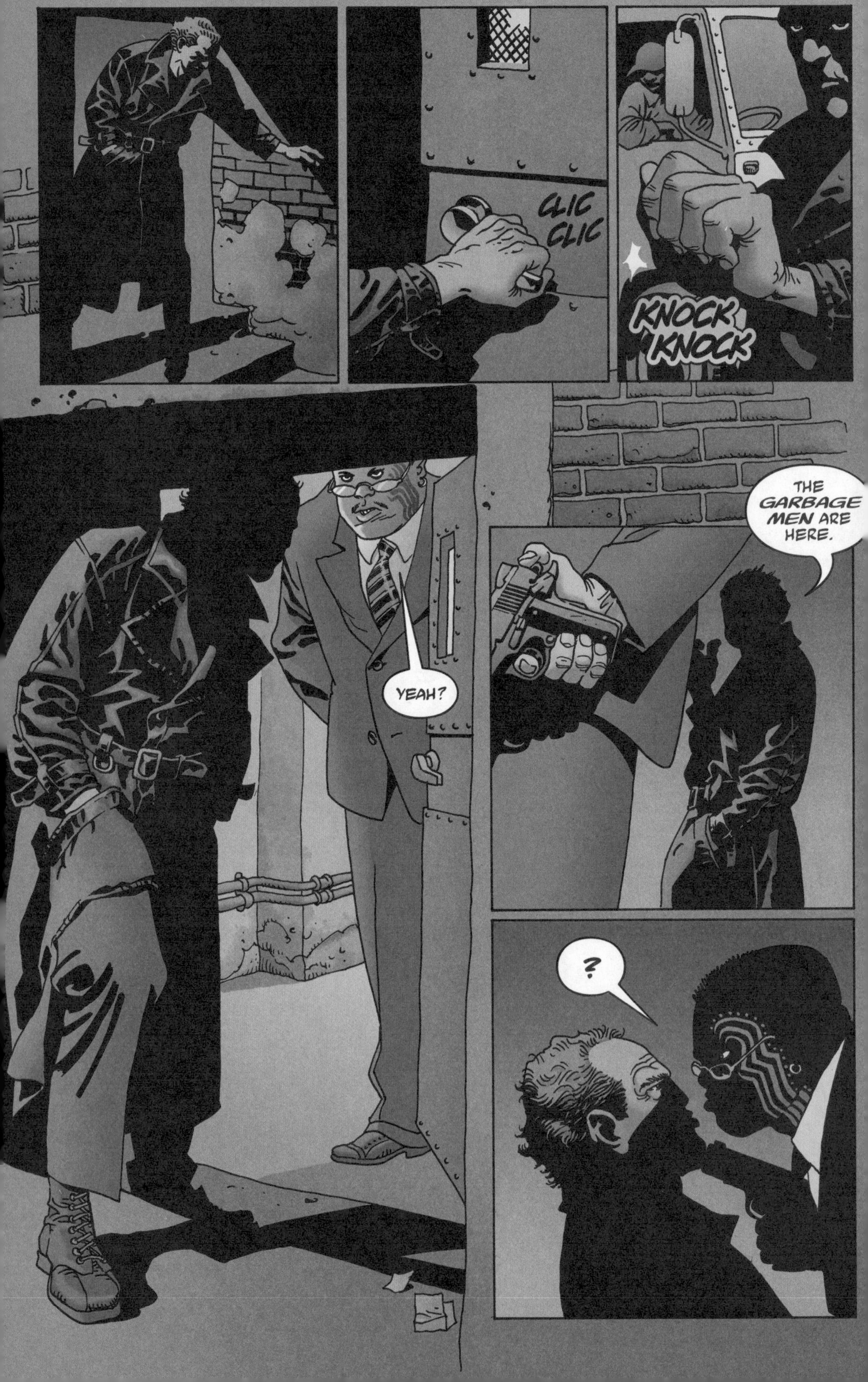

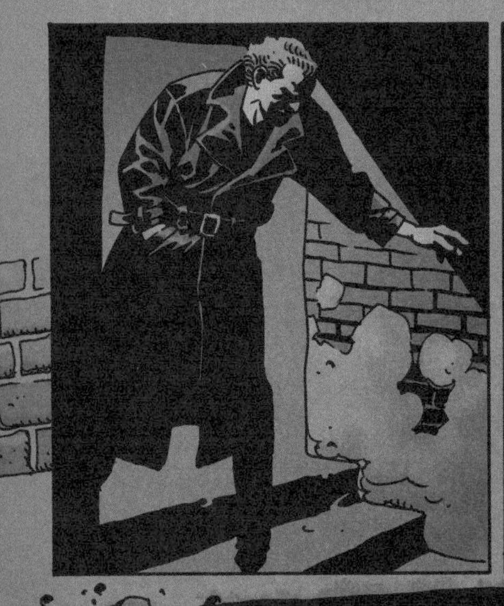

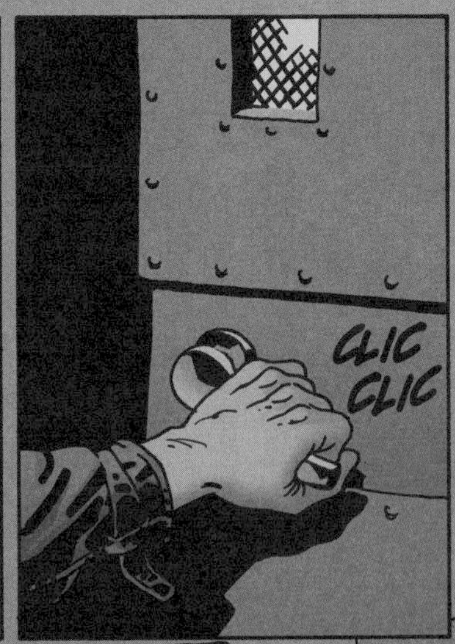
CLIC
CLIC

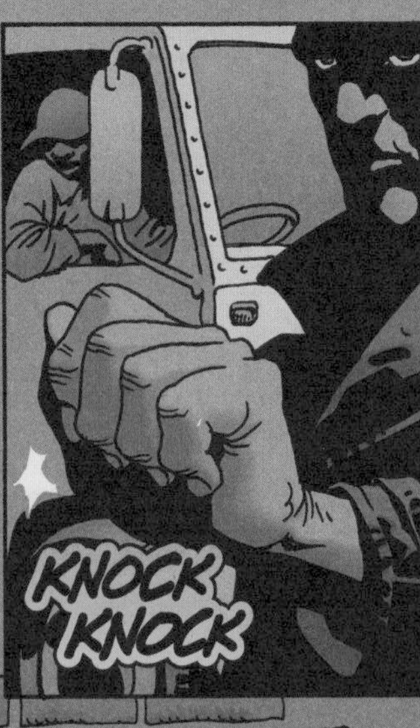
KNOCK
KNOCK

YEAH?

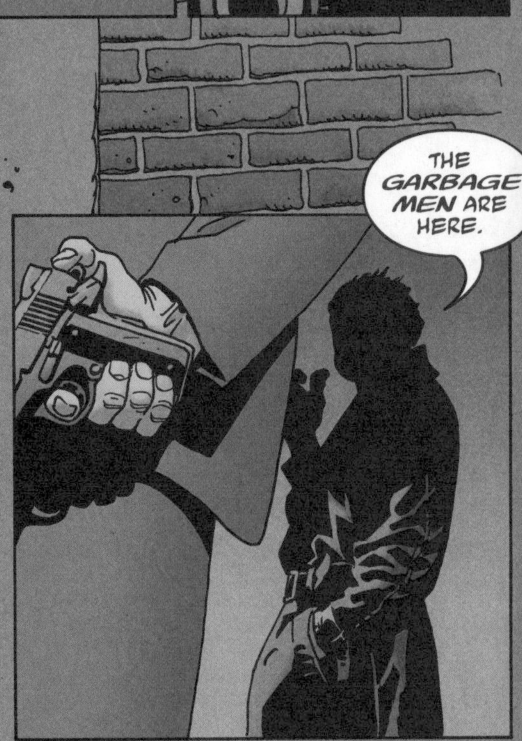
THE GARBAGE MEN ARE HERE.

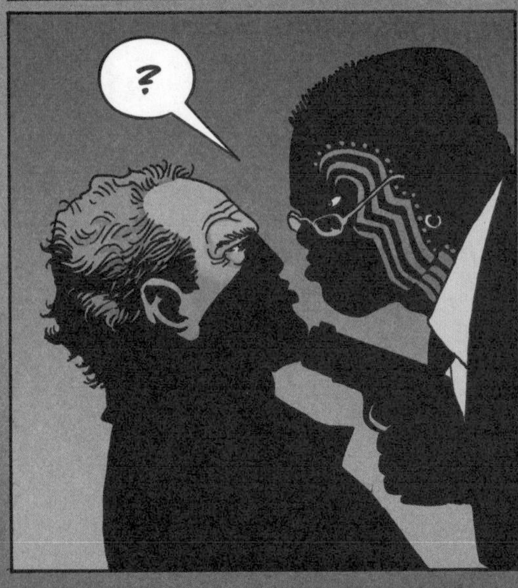
?

--YESTERDAY'S VIOLENCE THAT LEFT TWO CHILDREN CRITICALLY WOUNDED AND ONE DEAD.
WITNESSES ARE DESCRIBING THE SHOOTER AS ANOTHER CHILD, WHO AT THIS TIME...
...IS STILL AT LARGE.
WHO WAS THAT, RICO?
IT WAS ME.
WHERE'S RICO?
OUT BACK.
I WOULDN'T DO THAT IF I WERE YOU.
YOU'RE NOT ME.
I WOULDN'T WANT TO BE YOU RIGHT NOW, MR. ROTHSTEIN.

HMM. SOUNDS LIKE I DON'T WANT TO BE ME EITHER, DO I?
NO SIR, YOU DON'T.
WHO ARE YOU?
MY NAME'S SLAUGHTER.
HA! THAT'S QUITE A NAME.
WELL, WE DON'T GET TO PICK THEM, DO WE?
NO, NAMES AIN'T LIKE NOSES.
NO, THEY'RE NOT...
CRACK

"...BUT WE DO HAVE
TO LIVE UP TO THEM."
--THE MAYOR HAS PUT THE POLICE ON NOTICE THAT THE CITY WON'T TOLERATE LOSING ANY MORE CHILDREN TO GANG VIOLENCE.
ILLED IN
NTOWN
HEH.
GOOD LUCK WITH THAT.
WHY'S THAT FUNNY TO YOU, AGENT GRAVES?
IT'S NOT, DIZZY...
IT'S IMPOSSIBLE.
I FIND THAT FUNNY.
OR STUPID.
I FIND STUPID FUNNY.
STUPID MAKES ME SAD.
DOES IT? WHY?

BECAUSE FOLKS ACT STUPID WHEN THAT'S THEIR ONLY *CHOICE.*

BULLSHIT. PEOPLE ARE STUPID BECAUSE IT'S *EASY.*

BECAUSE THEY *DON'T WANT* TO CHOOSE. WHAT THEY DON'T UNDERSTAND IS...

...BEING STUPID *IS* A *CHOICE.* ADMIRING THE SILVER PLATTER... IGNORING THE SHIT HEAPED ON TOP OF IT...

HOT

CAB 723

Illinois
423 3784
Land of Lincoln

YER *FULL* OF IT.

?
STUPID MAKES *YOU* SAD, TOO.

THAT'S FUNNY.
"ANGRY? FUCK *RIGHT* I AM--"

--YOUR BOY PIP POPPED THE WRONG KID, GRAVY.
WAS YOU TOL' ME THAT THE MUTHAFUCKA'S SMART.
WELL, HE WASN'T FUCKIN' SMART ENOUGH TO TELL THE DIFF'RENCE 'TWEEN A NIGGA CURB-SERVIN' AN' A SHORTY COMIN' HOME FROM SCHOOL.
JUSTICE FOR ALL NO MORE KILLIN
TAKE BACK OUR STREETS
STOP
STOP THE VIOLENCE
JUSTICE FOR ALL
DON' FUCKIN' TELL ME TO RELAX, NIGGA! FUCKIN' TELL ME YER GONNA FIX THIS 'FORE FIVE-OH ROLLS UP ON HIS ASS.
STOP THE VIOLENCE
TAKE BACK OUR STREETS
YEAH--TALK TO HIS CREW--THAT'S A FINE IDEA. AN' DON' BE DRAGGIN' BALLS...
CLIC
...DUMB BITCH.

YOU--THIS YER FAULT--YOU AN' YOUR KIND, PUSHIN' POISON ON OUR STREETS--
TEACHIN' OUR BOYS THE ONLY WAY TO BE A MAN IS TO ACT A GANGSTER!
ME?
I DON' THINK SO.
JUSTICE FOR ALL
STOP THE
STOP THE
JUSTICE FOR ALL
STOP
STOP
YOU SEE THAT CAR?--THAT'S THE PO-LICE IN THAT CAR.
A LITTLE BROTHA IS DEAD. I'M HERE 'CAUSE I CARE.
STOP
STOP
STOP
STOP THE
AKS THEM IF THEY DO--THEN BE SURE TO LOOK IN THEIR EYES...
FOR THE TRUTH

NOK NOK
GO AWAY! I DONE SAID ALL I'M GONNA!
YOU AIN'T TALKED TO ME YET, MIZ HUFF.
YOUR BOY PIPPEN, HE'S A GOOD LITTLE MAN.
I GOT NOTHIN'...
I DON' WANT NOTHIN' FROM YOU. I WANNA HELP PIP.
HELP YOU, TOO.
MAY I COME IN?
"TAKE WHATEVER YOU WANT!"

THAT'S A FINE OFFER, MR. ROTHSTEIN. I APPRECIATE IT.
NOT THE REASON I'M HERE, THOUGH.
THEN WHY?
ROCKET LAUNCHER
YOU HAVE CHILDREN?
THEY'RE NOT CHILDREN ANYMORE. IS ONE OF THEM BEHIND--
NO. NO, NOTHING LIKE THAT. I'VE NEVER MET ANY A'YOUR KIDS.
Z Co.
"WHATEVER YOU'RE BEING PAID, I CAN DOUBLE IT IF YOU LEAVE."
"I ALREADY ACCEPTED THE JOB I HAVE. IF I WALKED AWAY FROM IT, WHAT WOULD THAT MAKE ME?"
"SMART."
NAH. THAT WOULD MAKE ME HAVING TO BE LEAVING FOR THE REST OF MY LIFE.
THE REST?--YOU STUPID SONOFABITCH--I'M SO CONNECTED MY FOOT IS KNEE-DEEP UP YOUR ASS RIGHT NOW.

BOOM
I KNOW YOU ARE CONNECTED. LOCAL, CIA, FBI-- EVEN HIGHER. I KNOW. WHAT I'M HERE FOR...

"...IS A DISCONNECT."
PIP'S IN A LOT OF TROUBLE.
DON'CHOO THINK I KNOW THAT?

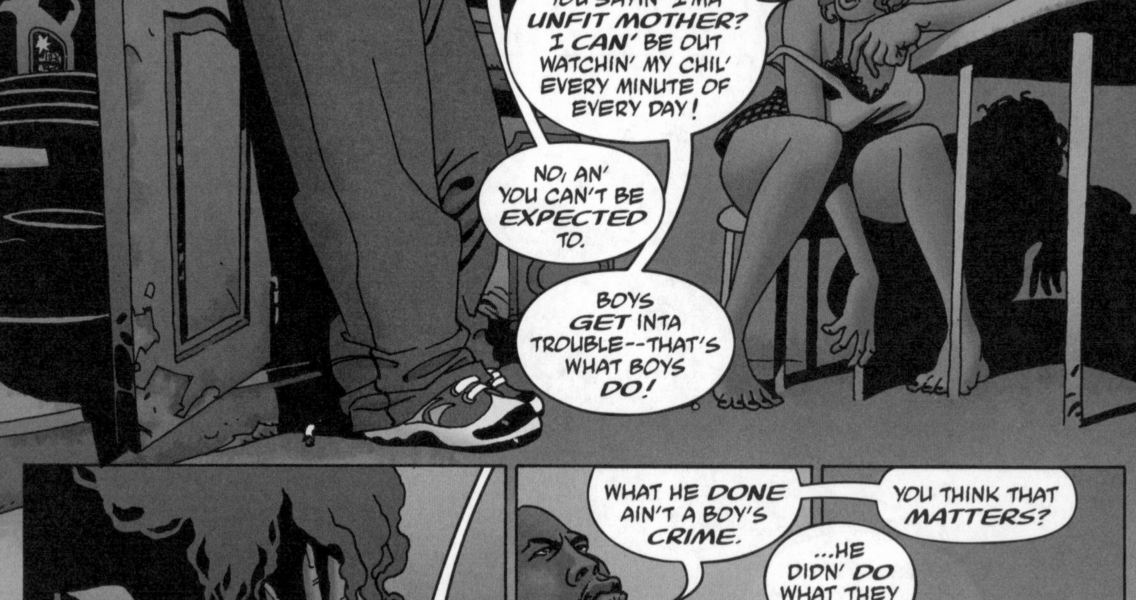

I'M SORRY, I KNOW YOU DO.
WHAT? YOU SAYIN' I'MA UNFIT MOTHER? I CAN' BE OUT WATCHIN' MY CHIL' EVERY MINUTE OF EVERY DAY!
NO, AN' YOU CAN'T BE EXPECTED TO.
BOYS GET INTA TROUBLE--THAT'S WHAT BOYS DO!

THE POLICE WILL PUT HIM IN PRISON.
HE'S JUST A BOY!

WHAT HE DONE AIN'T A BOY'S CRIME.
YOU THINK THAT MATTERS?
...HE DIDN' DO WHAT THEY SAID.

I GOT PEOPLE, DOWN SOUTH, HE CAN GO THERE, INSTEAD OF A CELL.
HE AIN'T BEEN HOME.
THAT MUST MAKE YOU HURT.
YOU SHOULD FIND HIM, AND TELL HIM WHAT I CAN DO FOR HIM.
IF I LEAVE--
YOU HAVE TO BE CAREFUL-- THE POLICE, THEY BE WATCHING YOU.
I DON' KNOW WHERE PIP IS--AN' I DON' KNOW WHAT TO DO!
I KNOW, THE HURT, IT'S HARD.
SO THINK ON WHERE HE MIGHT BE...

I ALWAYS THOUGHT I'D DIE IN BED.
YOU HAVE ONE HERE?
NO.
TELL ME... WHO'D I PISS OFF?
YOU? MR. ROTHSTEIN...
YOU. DIDN'T PISS OFF ANYBODY.

YES, MR. SLAUGHTER?
ROTHSTEIN IS DEAD. THE CONNECTION IS CUT.
NO MORE ATTACHÉS, NO MORE REVENGE...
NO MORE HUNDRED BULLETS.
GRAVES' GAME IS OVER.

"THAT'S GOOD NEWS."
"NO, IT'S JUST NEWS."
"HOW DO YOU THINK AGENT GRAVES WILL TAKE IT?"
"LIKE HE'S BEEN SLAPPED IN THE FACE BY HIS OWN MOTHER."

"ENDING
HIS GAME?
"MAKES
GRAVES THE
SOUREST
MAN ALIVE."

JOHNSON

NICE DAY, HUH?

WHAT?
I SAID IT'S A NICE DAY.

I *HEARD* YOU, IT'S JUST...
WHY THE FUCK WOULD YOU *SAY* THAT?

"THE SUN'S OUT, THE SKY'S BLUE-- BECAUSE IT *IS*.
SCENIC VIEW
½ MILE
"CAN'T I SAY IT'S A NICE DAY IF IT'S A *GODDAMN* NICE DAY?"

SURE, *I* DON'T FUCKIN' CARE... IT'S JUST NOT LIKE YOU TO ***NOTICE***.

MAYBE I NOTICE A ***LOT*** OF THINGS I DON'T MENTION.

MAYBE YOU DO.
PULL OFF UP HERE.

Y'KNOW WE'RE BOTH FUCKIN' RONIN NOW.
SCENIC VIEW
YOU OKAY WITH THAT?
I GUESS.
NO.
YEAH, HE DID. ON YOUR BOSS'S ORDER.
WELL...I DIDN'T FEEL GOOD ABOUT THAT.
I REACTED. IT WAS REFLEXES.
THE KID WENT FOR HIS GUN--
THANKS, BY THE WAY.

DON'T.
I CAN'T TELL YOU I'M FUCKIN' GRATEFUL?
ARE YOU?
...I COULD OF HANDLED IT MYSELF.
IT'S THE THOUGHT THAT COUNTS, THOUGH.
YOU THINK YOU KNOW WHAT I'M THINKING?
POP
I KNOW YOU THINK IT'S A NICE DAY...

GET UP, LOOP...
WE'RE TAKING A WALK.
"100 BULLETS"
CHAPTER IV: OUR MEN IN THE RAVINE

BD-RING
"YES?"
BD-RING
"JAVIER?"
YES.
I'VE JUST RECEIVED NEWS THAT CONCERNS ME.
THAT'S NOT SURPRISING. I IMAGINE MOST NEWS DOES...
...BEING WHO YOU ARE.
WELL, I'D LIKE TO KNOW WHY.
I HAVE NO IDEA. PERHAPS YOUR INFLATED EGO MIGHT, THOUGH.

...
ABE ROTHSTEIN IS DEAD--PROFESSIONALLY, FROM WHAT I'VE BEEN TOLD. ARE YOU SAYING YOU HAD NOTHING TO DO WITH IT?
WHY WOULD I?
SO YOU ARE RESPONSIBLE. IN GOD'S NAME--
AUGUSTUS--WE HAD AN AGREEMENT--
--WE'VE HAD MANY--AND YOU DISAGREE TEN MINUTES AFTER MAKING THEM.
CHRIST, JAVIER, AFTER ALL THESE YEARS I KNOW YOU ONLY THINK OF YOURSELF--WHAT'S BEST FOR YOU.
THAT PUTS ME IN RATHER ELITE COMPANY, DOESN'T IT?
I HAD NOTHING TO DO WITH ROTHSTEIN'S DEATH. THOUGH...
...I DON'T DISAGREE WITH WHOEVER DID.
OF COURSE YOU DON'T.
IT'S SIMPLE...

FUCK
PHIL
GRAVES...
...OR HE WILL FUCK YOU.
IT'S THAT SIMPLE.
REALLY?
REALLY THAT SIMPLE. HE FEELS FUCKED-- HE'S ALWAYS FELT FUCKED.
WHY DO YOU THINK THAT?
BECAUSE HE'S DONE WHAT WAS ASKED.
I DON'T FOLLOW YOU...
NO...
...NOR I YOU.

CLICK
MAXIMO GOMEZ
JAVIER...
YOU SONOFABITCH.
MAXIMO
BENITO, CONTACT LONO.
TELL HIM...
MAXIMO GOMEZ PA

...WE'RE GOING TO SEATTLE.

SHIT...
WHAT?
I STEPPED IN IT.
WHAT?
SHIT.
WHAT KIND?
I DON'T KNOW... WE'RE IN THE FUCKIN' WOODS...
ANIMAL SHIT. 'LESS...
...YOU DIDN' CRAP YERSELF, AN' HAVE IT ROLLED DOWN YER LEG, DID'JA, BROTHER?
FUCK YOU.
I MEAN, THAT WOULD BE A SOLID LAST ACT OF DEFIANCE...
GETTIN' YER SHIT ON MY SHOES.
I'LL HAVE TO REMEMBER THAT.
WALK.
"YO, GRAVY..."

S'UP, DAWG?
I AIN'T'CHER DAWG, MUTHAFUCKA, I'M YER MUTHAFUCKIN' BOSS.
A'IGHT, A'IGHT. S'UP...
BOSS?
YOU SPEAK AT PIP'S CREW?
I AM AS WE SPEAK. THEY AIN'T SNITCHIN'.
FUCK, YEAH.
FER REAL? YOU THREATEN TO DROP SOME SHIT?
I'M TALKIN' SERIOUS "DON' FUCK WIT' ME" SHIT.
HARDCORE SHIT, DAW--
...BOSS.
GET PAID?
I OFFERED.
AN' STILL?
AN' NAH.
DAMN. THE LITTLE BROTHAS 'ER TOUGH.
PUT ONE ON FO' ME.
YO, KEEN...

KEEN...

MY NAME IS LEON.

YOU KNOW WHAT THAT MEANS?

"I UNDERSTAN' YOU NEEDIN' TO PROTEC' PIPPEN, I DO.

"AN' I RESPECT THAT, AN' YOU, FER DOIN' IT.

"IS ADMIR'BLE.

"...HIS MOMS GAVE HIS ASS UP...

"SO I DON' NEED FER YOU TO TELL ME WHERE YER DAWG IS HIDIN'...

"BUT I DO NEED YOU."

SO WHAT WENT DOWN IN ATLANTIC CITY... YOU THINK GRAVES WAS LYING TO US?
NO. BUT I'M PRETTY DAMN SURE HE WASN'T TELLING US ALL OF THE TRUTH.
OR, AND THIS IS WHAT REALLY HAS KIND OF PISSED ME OFF...
...HE CREATED THE TRUTH. HE MANIPULATED EVENTS AND PEOPLE INTO A PLACE HE NEEDED THEM AT...
AND HE DIDN'T DO IT ALONE.
HOW YOU KNOW THAT?
BECAUSE IT WOULD HAVE BEEN IMPOSSIBLE. HE'S GOT JUICE, BUT NOT THAT KIND.
NOT YET, ANYWAY.
Y'KNOW, JACK, YER RIGHT...

IT IS A NICE DAY.
FUCKIN' TAKIN' A WALK, OUT IN THE SUN, AFTER...

THIS SONOFABITCH TRIED TO KILL ME, DIDN'T HE?
LONO TOLD HIM TO.

LOOP?--LONO TELL YOU TO FUCKIN' KILL ME?

HE SAID, "KILL THE MOTHERFUCKER, BEFORE HE KILLS YOU."

GUESS YOU FUCKED *THAT*, HUH?

I'D SAY SO.

RUN.

BAM

YO PIP!

...THAT YOU, KEEN?

YEAH, SON, IS ME.

BAM
BAM
"I FUCKED UP, I KNOW, SERIOUS.
"I FUCKED UP."
"YEAH, WELL... YOU DIN' GET THE JOB DONE."
BAM
BAM
BAM
BAM
"JOB? FUCK THE JOB... HEAR ME...
"I FUCKED UP.
BAM
BAM
BAM
"I'M SCARED."
BAMBAMBAMBAM

JESUS H...WHAT THE FUCK'RE YOU TRYIN' TO *DO* HERE, HIGHJACK?

WHY DON' YOU JUS' SEND UP A *FLARE,* LET EVERY HILLBILLY AN' HIS SISTER KNOW WHERE WE ARE?

"FIVE-OH, I KNOW--THEY GONNA *GUN ME DOWN.*"

NAH DEY AIN'--I GOTCHA FUCKIN' BACK, BAD NEWZ!

GRAVY BEEN 'ROUN'?

HELL YEAH. MUTHAFUCKA'S *HANGRY.*

SHIT'S ALL BLOWED UP. NIGGA YOU SMOK'T WAS REAL GOOD AT *SCHOO'* N'SHIT.

I FUCKED UP.
STOP *SAYIN'* THAT.

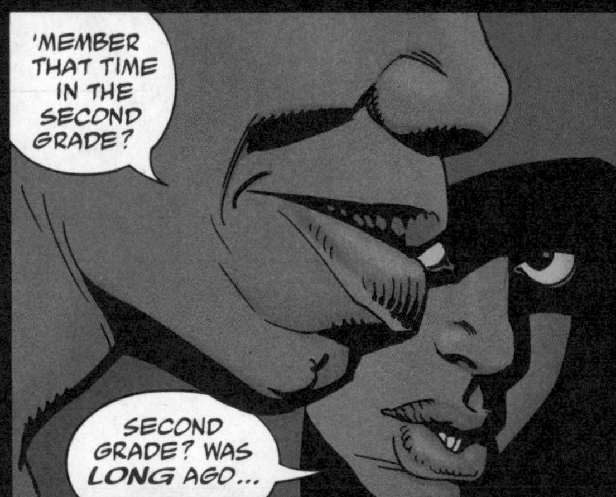

'MEMBER THAT TIME IN THE SECOND GRADE?
SECOND GRADE? WAS *LONG* AGO...

THAT TIME... YOU WAS IN THE SHIT, FER DRAWIN' ALL NASTY-ASS PIT'CHERS ON THE BOARD WHEN MIZZ LYNCH WAS OUT THE ROOM.
THEM GIANT PUSSIES, AN' THAT DUDE WIT' THE DICK, BIG AS *HE* WAS...
FRANKENSTEIN.

WHAT?
WAS FRANKENSTEIN. WITH THE BIG DICK. COME TO STICK IT IN ALL THE MUTHAFUCKIN' PUSSIES THERE WAS.

MIZZ LYNCH DRAGGED MY ASS STRAIGHT DOWN TO THE PRINCIPAL'S.

HE SAYS I WAS GONNA BE KICKED OUTTA SCHOO'. BROUGHT ME RIGHT BACK TO CLASS, SO HE COULD SEE THE EVIDENCE WIT' HIS OWN EYES...

BUT THERE WEREN'T NONE. I ERASED EVERYTHIN'.

THAT MADE ME FEEL LIKE MICHAEL.

LIKE YOU WAS MY PIPPEN.

KEEN, I AIN'T NEVER TELL NO ONE THIS...I AIN'T NAMED AFTER PIPPEN THE BALLER...

I'M NAMED AFTER PIPPIN THE PRINCE.

MY MOMS' FAVORITE VIDEO. WAS A STORY 'BOUT A BOY TRYIN' TO GET HAPPY.

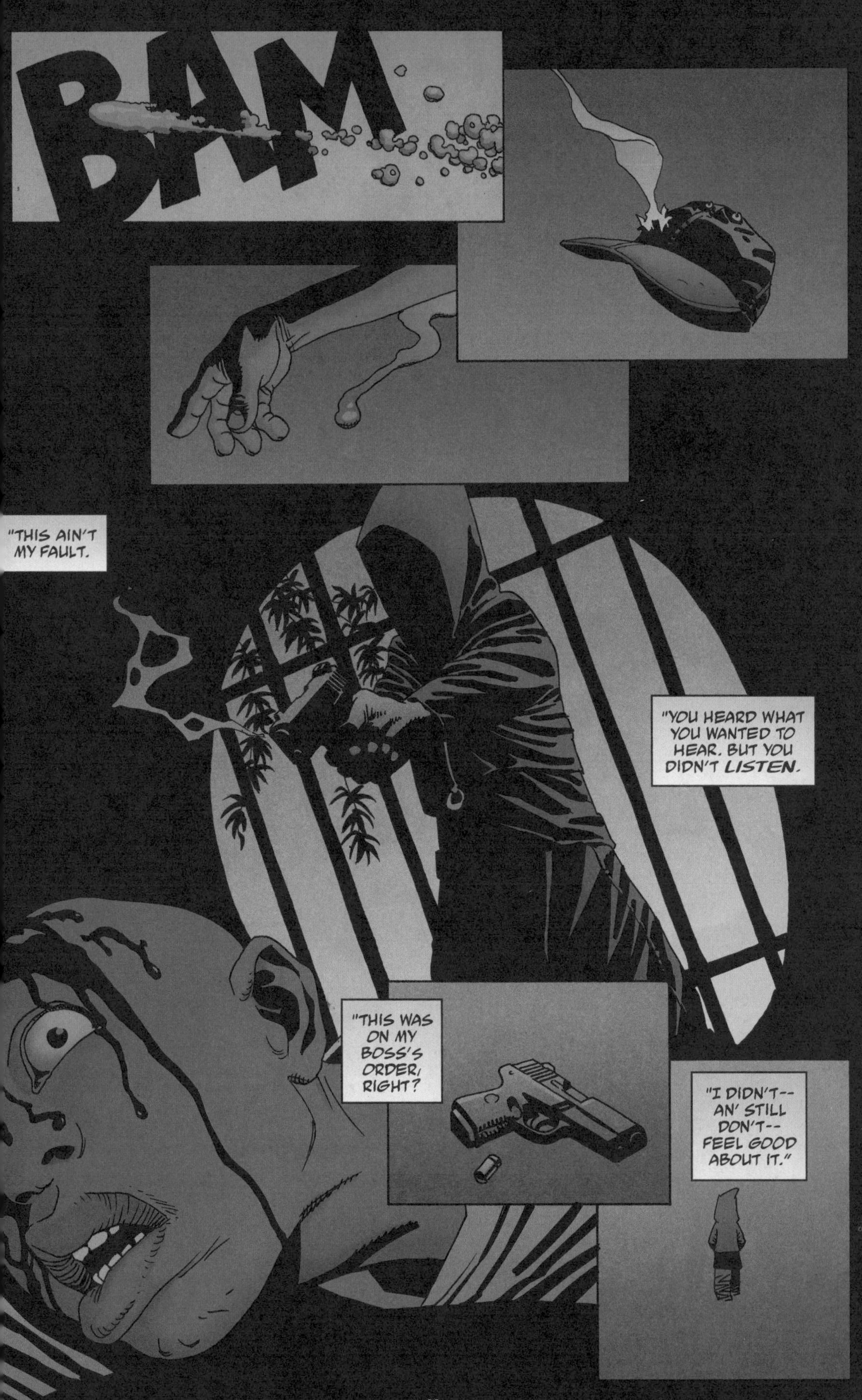
BAM
"THIS AIN'T MY FAULT.
"YOU HEARD WHAT YOU WANTED TO HEAR. BUT YOU DIDN'T LISTEN.
"THIS WAS ON MY BOSS'S ORDER, RIGHT?
"I DIDN'T-- AN' STILL DON'T-- FEEL GOOD ABOUT IT."

...YOU KNOW WHY?
BECAUSE HE DIDN'T ASK ME TO DO THE JOB, COLE.
RONIN?
WHAT THE FUCK YOU THINK GRAVES IS, ASSHOLE?

100
BULLETS
XIII
9mm x 19

--SEWER WORKERS DISCOVERED THE CHILD'S BODY EARLIER THIS MORNING IN A HYDE PARK TUNNEL...
NANCY BROWN IN THE SCENE
NEWS
The biggest NFL draft busts of the modern era - Kansas guard Chalme

AH, FER THE LOVE OF GOD...
TELL ME ABOUT IT. STORIES LIKE THAT WORRY ME ABOUT MY OWN KIDS. I JUST WANT TO HOLD 'EM, FUCKIN' NEVER LET GO.

WHAT?-- NO. JESUS, FUCKIN' JAG-OFF-- I'M TALKIN' ABOUT...

THE GUY CAN HARDLY BREATHE...

TAKE IT OUTSIDE.

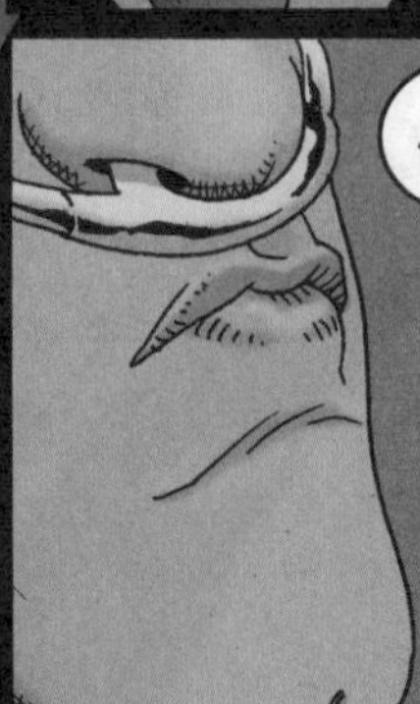

OH. YEAH.
SORRY, COOP.

I CAN BREATHE JUST FINE, LOU.
YOU CAN.
OCCURRED TO YOU THAT JUST 'CAUSE I CAN'T SMOKE ANYMORE, I MIGHT STILL LIKE THE SMELL?
NEWS
RACING
NO.
YOU CAN STILL SMELL IT? EVEN WITH THAT THING...
YEAH. THE SILENT FARTS YOU SQUEEZE OUT, TOO.
SHIT.
WORSE. YOU SHOULD SEE A DOCTOR.
I'M FINE.
SO AM I.

NOT REALLY WHY--IT'S BECAUSE YOU'RE SCARED TO BE ME.
IT'S OKAY. IT'S GOOD, ACTUALLY.
DONUTS
I DON'T GET WHY YOU HAVEN'T RETIRED. I WOULD OF.
WELL, YOU'RE NOT ME. I'VE BEEN WITH THIS FAMILY...SHIT... I NEED TO BE HERE.
WE SECURE?
CRZZ--MISS D'ARCY IS A BLOCK

"100 BULLETS"

CHAPTER FIVE: ROOSTER

AYE, BOSS.
REMI. I HOPE YOU'RE CALLING ME WITH GOOD NEWS.
WHY'S THAT?
I COULD USE SOME.
OKAY. HOW ABOUT JOAN D'ARCY WILL BE DEAD IN AN HOUR? I'VE BEEN WAITING FOR HER TO SHOW UP TO HER GOLD COAST DIGS FOR A FEW DAYS--
--WAITING?
YOU GOT IT-- NOT CHASIN'. ALL BY YOUR BOOK. STAKE THE FUCK OUT, AND EVENTUALLY WHO YER AFTER WILL WALK INTO THE BULLET MEANT FOR THEM.
CALL ME IN AN HOUR.
CLIC

B-DEEP
B-DEEP
B-DEEP
HOME
HEY MA, I CAN'T **TALK** RIGHT NOW...
REMI? IT'S NOT YER MOTHER, IT'S **AUNT LINDI.**
AUNT LINDI? WHAT'S GOIN' ON? WHAT'RE YOU--
YER MOTHER, REMI...
MEDI
OH BABY, SHE HAD A **HEART ATTACK.**
"YOU DON'T **LOOK** SO GOOD, AGENT GRAVES."
HOME

REALLY?
DO I LOOK SICK, OR DO I LOOK BAD, DIZZY?
BAD.
GOOD.
I WANT YOU TO WAIT OUT HERE.
WHY?
BECAUSE WHAT JAVIER AND I HAVE TO SAY ISN'T YOUR CONCERN.
--YET, YOU MEAN.
IF ANYBODY GIVES YOU THE SLIGHTEST HARD TIME...

"...DROP THEM."
WHAT AM I DOIN' HERE?
YOUR JOB, LONO...
IS THAT A PROBLEM?
NOT AT ALL. BUT I DON'T NEED YOU HERE TO DO IT, AUGUSTUS. IN FACT, YOU SHOULDN'T BE--
DON'T TELL ME ABOUT ME, CLEAR?
I HOPE TO WORK THIS OUT MYSELF.
I REALLY WANT TO WORK THIS OUT MYSELF. BUT IF I CAN'T...
...YOU'LL BE WAITING OUTSIDE.

WE HAVEN'T HAD ANY INCIDENTS SINCE YOU'VE BEEN OUT OF TOWN, MISS D'ARCY, WHICH IS GOOD.
AND OUR SOURCES PUT GRAVES ON THE WEST COAST, AS OF YESTERDAY.
THAT'S VERY GOOD, AND WHY I'M BACK.
UNDERSTOOD. THOUGH WE STILL FEEL--
JOANIE!
COOP!
HOW ARE YOU?
I'M--
...YOU FIRST.

I'M FINE, KIDDO.
REALLY?
REALLY.
I WORRY ABOUT YOU.
YOU SHOULD WORRY ABOUT YOU--LIKE I DO.
48
LIKE YOU GET PAID TO.
NO, KIDDO--I GET PAID TO PROTECT. WORRYING I DO ON MY OWN DIME.
I KNOW.
IT'S SO GOOD TO SEE YOU AGAIN. I FEEL SAFE WHEN YOU'RE AROUND.
"I WORRY LESS, WHEN YOU ARE..."
"YER MOTHER'S ON HER WAY TO UNIVERSITY HOSPITAL. THEY GOT GOOD DOCTORS THERE, I HEAR."

AUNT LINDI, THERE AIN'T NO SUCH--
...
YOU GOIN' WITH HER?
OF COURSE I'M GOIN'! NOT IN THE AMBULANCE THOUGH. THEY SAID I COULDN'T.

WHO SAID?
THE PARAMEDICS, REMI! WHO YOU THINK?
LISTEN-- YOU MAKE SURE YOU CALL ME ABOUT ANYTHING 'TIL I GET THERE.

WHEN YOU COMIN'?
RIGHT FUCKIN' NOW.

YOU SHOULDN' TALK LIKE THAT.
SORRY.

AUNT LINDI--MY MA HAD A FUC--

I'LL BE THERE AS SOON AS I CAN.

J 5 3

STOP

--AM
LOU--
WHAT DO WE GOT?!
LONE GUNMAN, COMING AT TWELVE O'CLO--
BAM
BAM BAM
BAM
LOCK IT DOWN, LYLE!
ON IT, BOSS!
JOANIE...LET'S GO--WE'LL TAKE THE STAIRS DOWN TO THE PANIC ROOM--
BAM BAM
NOW!
BAMBAM

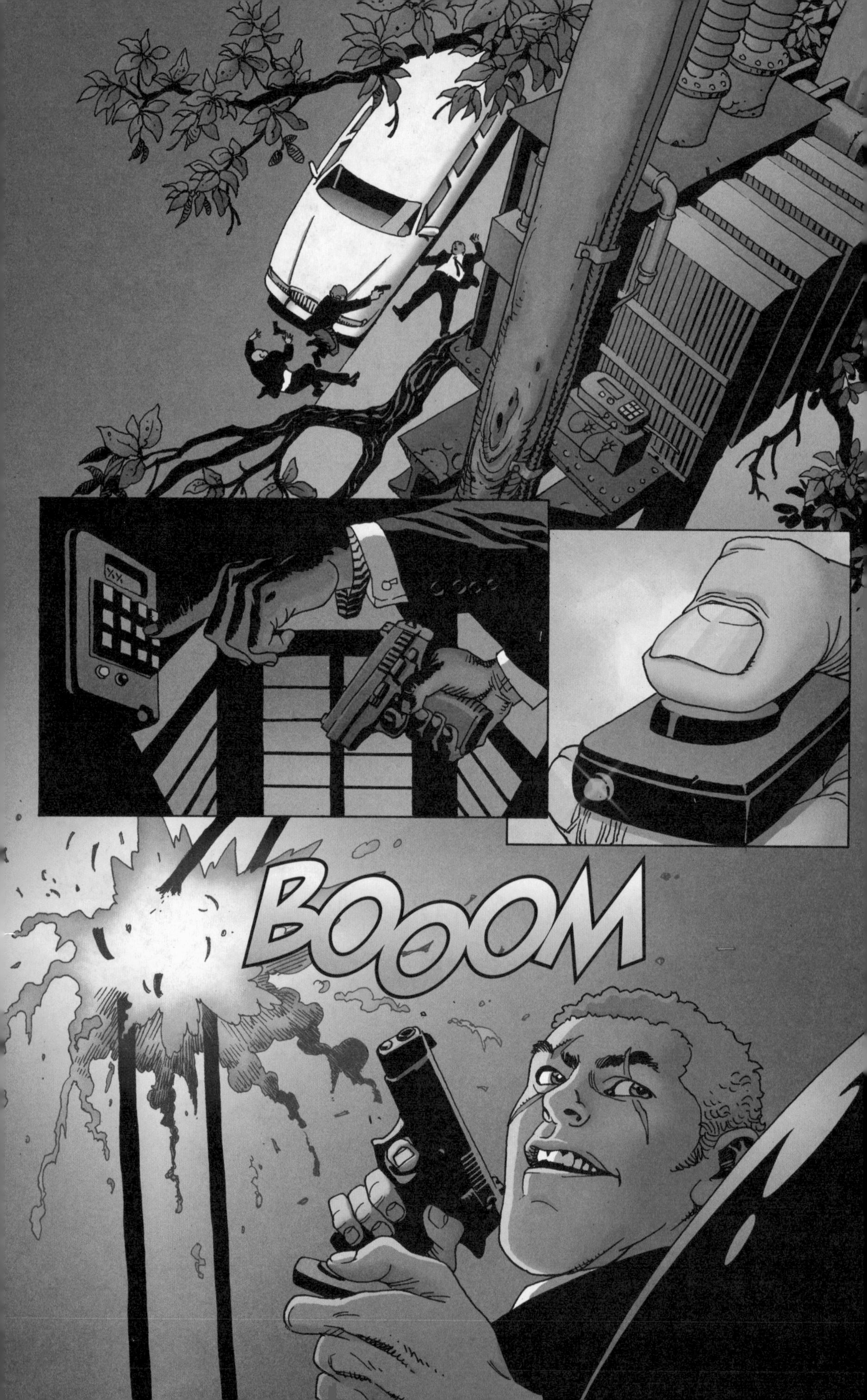
BOOOM

WHAT--
THE POWER'S BEEN CUT. DON'T WORRY, THE GENERATOR WILL KICK IN...

OR NOT.
GODDAMNIT.

WE'VE GOT YOU COVERED, MR. COOPER. THERE'S AN AUXILIARY GENERATOR IN THE PANIC ROOM.

COOP...

I WON'T LET THIS MANIAC HURT YOU.

...
IT'S A MINUTEMAN, COOP.

"YOU SAY THERE'S A DIFFERENCE? I DON'T.
"I'VE KILLED PEOPLE, JOANIE-- AND THEY ALL HAUNT ME.
"EVEN THE ONES I DID IN THE MARINES...
K35
"BODIES I NEVER SAW.
K35
"BUT MY MIND, AFTER A TIME, CREATED FACES FOR."

"I GO TO BED WITH MY FACES EVERY NIGHT. EVERY DAMN ONE.
"AND I THANK GOD FOR LETTING ME DO SO.
FWAASSH
"BUT THERE AIN'T NO GOD IN THE MINUTEMEN. AND IF THERE IS?...
"...HE'S A BITCH I WOULDN'T RECOGNIZE.
"GODDAMNIT..."

...WE'VE BEEN *HACKED.*
OH, JESUS... COOP...HE'S GONNA *KILL* YOU.

GET IN THE BATHROOM.
OVER MY DEAD *BODY.*

NO. I *WON'T* DIE IN A--

--GET IN THE GODDAMN TOILET!

...PLEASE, MISS D'ARCY.

OKAY, FUCKERS...
...TIME TO GET FU--

BOOM

BD-RING
BD-RING

...SO JAVIER VASCO'S A *LIAR*.

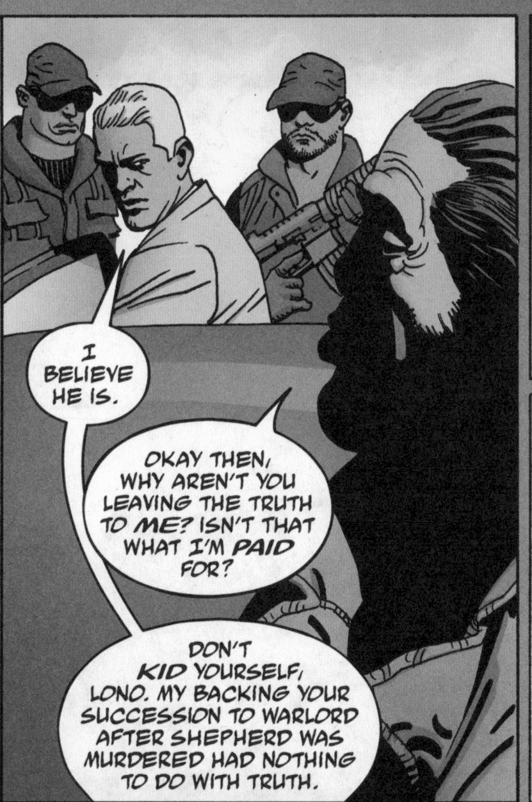

I BELIEVE HE IS.
OKAY THEN, WHY AREN'T YOU LEAVING THE TRUTH TO *ME*? ISN'T THAT WHAT I'M *PAID* FOR?
DON'T *KID* YOURSELF, LONO. MY BACKING YOUR SUCCESSION TO WARLORD AFTER SHEPHERD WAS MURDERED HAD NOTHING TO DO WITH TRUTH.

THE *TRUTH* IS, YOU OWE YOUR POSITION TO THE TRUTH THAT YOUR...

--*UNPREDICTABILITY*-- SCARES THE *SHIT* OUT OF PEOPLE.

IF JAVIER'S LYING, I'LL KNOW. THAT'S WHY I'M HERE.
TO LOOK IN HIS EYES.
WHAT WORRIES ME--AND SHOULD WORRY YOU AS WELL--IS IF HE'S BEING HONEST.
ARE YOU LISTENING?
HUH?-- YEAH. HONEST.
I'M JUST MARKING THE ORDER.
JUST WHAT?
IN CASE.

"100 BULLETS"

CHAPTER SIX: KILL DE SAC

MR. VASCO, YOU HAVE A VISITOR.
I'LL BE UP IN A FEW MINUTES OR SO...
HE CAN WAIT.
NO...
...I CAN'T.
GRAVES?
I WASN'T EXPECTING YOU...
ERGH

HOLD YOUR FIRE!
CLIK
CLIK
CLIK
SMART, CAPTAIN. VERY SMART.
NOBODY WANTS TO DIE HERE.
ESPECIALLY NOT OLD MEN.
OLD?
SPEAK FOR YOURSELF, PHIL.

'SCUSE ME...
GOTTA LIGHT?
I DON'T SMOKE.
GIMME TIME, CHICA...
...I JUST GOT HERE.
SO, YER WHAT--VASCO'S MISTRESS? THAT MUST SUCK. SUCKIN' THE LIFE OUTTA--
WHDO

NO SHIT?
YOU CREW? WELL, FUCK ME...
I MEAN, LOOKIN' AROUND, ALL I CAUGHT WAS A BUNCH A' ASS CLOWNS.
YEAH...
ME, TOO.
YOU, BABY DOLL, ARE GOIN' SOMEWHERE YOU DON'T WANT TO.
WRONG, LOVERBOY. I'M NOT GOING ANYWHERE.
"I APOLOGIZE."

PHIL SAYS HE'S SORRY.
I'M SORRY, TOO. --YOU?
WELL THEN IF WE ALL ARE...
...WE CAN GET FUCKING DOWN TO BUSINESS, BECAUSE THAT'S WHERE WE ALL NEED TO BE.
IT SEEMS, PHIL, YOU AND I CAME HERE FOR THE SAME REASON.
THAT SAYS SOMETHING ABOUT YOUR CHARACTER, JAVIER--BOTH OF US JUMPING TO THE SAME CONCLUSION.
AND NOTHING OF YOUR OWN, OF COURSE.

I TOLD AUGUSTUS, AND I'LL TELL YOU THE SAME: I HAD NO HAND IN ABE ROTHSTEIN'S DEATH.
WELL, SOMEONE'S HAS BLOOD ON THEM...
NOT YOURS THOUGH, HMM? THEY STAY CLEAN WHILE THAT HIGH HORSE YOU'RE ON WADES THROUGH THE RED RIVER?
JESUS, PHIL...I MEAN, WHAT DID YOU EXPECT?
OUR CONTRACT TO BE HONORED.
WHAT ARE YOU, A LITTLE GIRL IN THE BACK SEAT FOR THE FIRST TIME?--THAT'S NAIVE.

LORD
LINE
FINE WINE
...THERE'S NO HONOR AMONG THIEVES.
HEH.
HA.
HAHAHAHA
"SO YOU CAME IN THAT CAR..."

I'M IN THE ONE ON ITS ASS.

YEAH, I SAW YOU GET OUT AFTER A MAN.

HA. BABY, YER A REAL PISTOL.

I AIN'T NO BABY.

NO, YOU AIN'T. YER A HOT PIECE OF ASS--

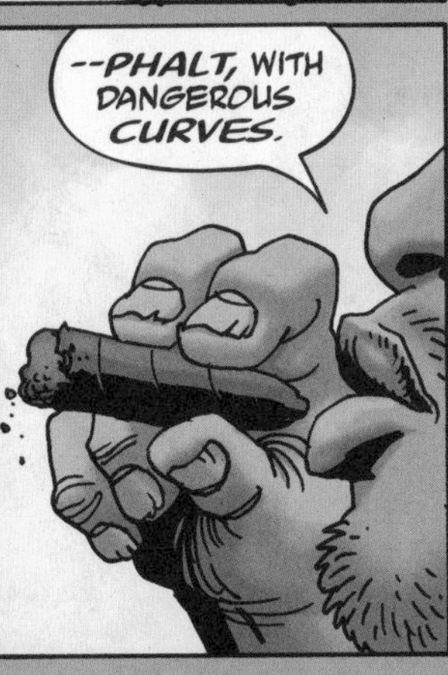
--PHALT, WITH DANGEROUS CURVES.

WHAT THE FUCK IS YER STORY?

HOW THE HELL DO I KNOW? I'M IN IT.

DON' I KNOW THAT.

YEAH, PISTOL--WE RIDE IN CARS, BUT WE DON' DRIVE 'EM.

THAT SOUNDS LIKE SOMETHIN' SOMEONE ELSE I KNEW WOULDA SAID.

HE WAS SPOT ON.

WHAT MAKES YOU THINK HE WAS A HE?

HMM. POINT. IT IS A CHICK SORTA VIEW.

YOU'LL KILL ME IF YOU TELL ME YER INTO THE PUSSY, PISTOL.

I MIGHT KILL YOU ANYWAY...

AND MY NAME IS DIZZY.

DO YOU REMEMBER THE NIGHTS WE USED TO SPEND DOWN HERE?
THE DETAILS? NOT REALLY.
ONLY THAT THEY WERE LONG...
SERIOUSLY?-- ALL THE BEGINNINGS OF YOUR "BETTER FUTURE" BULLSHIT?
NOT BULL, FUCK, HORSE, OR CHICKEN SHIT, BUT TRUTH.
BUT YOU DON'T REMEMBER OUR CONVERSATIONS?
I HAVE AN IMPRESSION AS TO WHAT I THINK THEY WERE ABOUT, AS OPPOSED TO WHAT THEY REALLY MIGHT HAVE BEEN.
IT'S BETTER THAT WAY... CLEARER, NOT REMEMBERING THE DETAILS.
I CLING TO THAT, I GUESS. THE THREE OF US.

YOU MEAN YOU, AND THE TWO OF US.

NO...THE TWO OF US AND YOU IS WHAT I MEAN.
OR JUST ME.

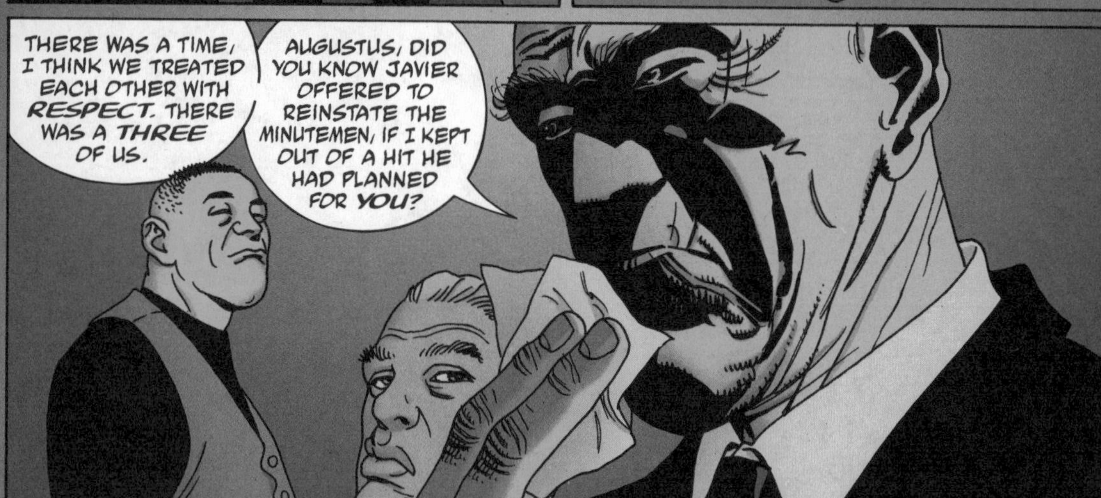

THERE WAS A TIME, I THINK WE TREATED EACH OTHER WITH RESPECT. THERE WAS A THREE OF US.
AUGUSTUS, DID YOU KNOW JAVIER OFFERED TO REINSTATE THE MINUTEMEN, IF I KEPT OUT OF A HIT HE HAD PLANNED FOR YOU?

I DID KEEP AWAY, BUT NOT FOR THAT REASON.

AND JAVIER, DO YOU KNOW AUGUSTUS HAS NO USE FOR YOU?

YES...

"...BUT THAT'S WHY I'M STILL ALIVE, NO?"
DIZZY...
DIZZY, DIZZY, DIZZY.
IT FITS.
I GOT A MESSAGE FER YOU. FROM THAT SPOT-ON DUDE...
...SHEPHERD, WASN'T IT?
HOW--
--WE TALKED, WHILE HE WAS BLEEDIN' OUT IN THE DESERT. HE TOLD ME TO TELL YOU...

IT WASN'T YOUR FAULT.
I STILL BLAME MYSELF.
YEAH, WELL...
I BLAME YOU, TOO.
"SO...HERE WE ARE RIGHT BACK WHERE WE STARTED."

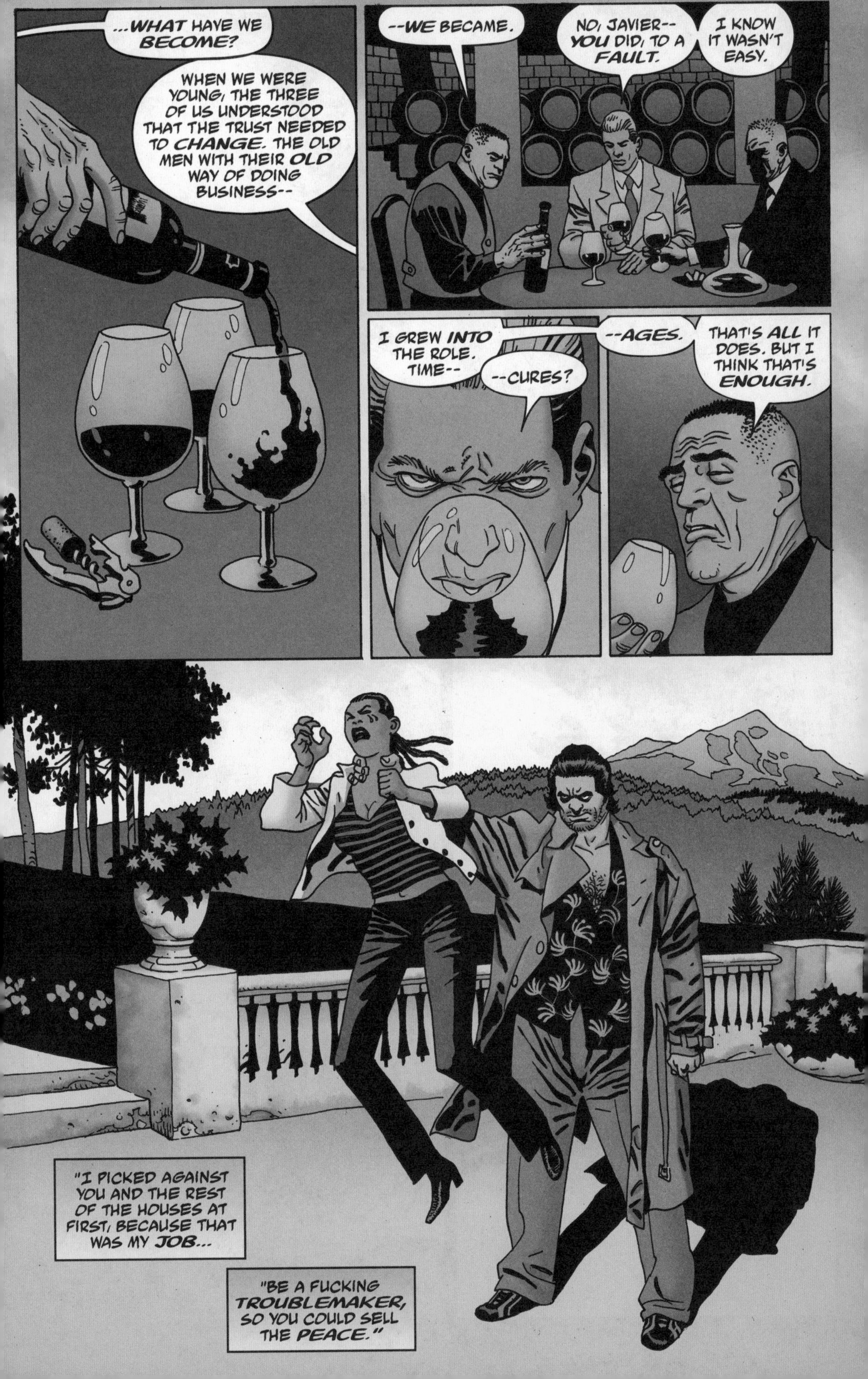

...*WHAT* HAVE WE *BECOME?*

WHEN WE WERE YOUNG, THE THREE OF US UNDERSTOOD THAT THE TRUST NEEDED TO *CHANGE.* THE OLD MEN WITH THEIR *OLD* WAY OF DOING BUSINESS--

--*WE* BECAME.

NO, JAVIER-- *YOU* DID, TO A *FAULT.*

I KNOW IT WASN'T EASY.

I GREW *INTO* THE ROLE. TIME--

--CURES?

--*AGES.*

THAT'S *ALL* IT DOES. BUT I THINK THAT'S *ENOUGH.*

"I PICKED AGAINST YOU AND THE REST OF THE HOUSES AT FIRST, BECAUSE THAT WAS MY *JOB*...

"BE A FUCKING *TROUBLEMAKER,* SO YOU COULD SELL THE *PEACE.*"

"AS I GREW OLDER, I REALIZED THAT CONFLICT WITHIN THE TRUST WAS ITS BLOOD. IT KEPT US HONEST, AND THE PEACE WE AGREED UPON AS YOUNG MEN...
"...WAS BAD FOR ITS HEART."
"THAT SO? OR BECAUSE YOU FELT GUILT IN YOUR OWN?"
"AUGUSTUS, WHY DO YOU THINK I NEVER HAD ANY CHILDREN?"
"I ALWAYS THOUGHT YOU DIDN'T HAVE THE BALLS, JAVIER."

JUST THE BRAINS.
GRAVES-- WE MADE IT CLEAR IN THE TRUST THAT ROTHSTEIN WAS *OFF LIMITS...*

"EVEN *AFTER* YOU SURFACED.

"DESPITE WHAT HE PROVIDED TO YOU, HE WAS MORE VALUABLE TO US *ALIVE.*"

AUGUSTUS, YOU ACCUSED *ME,* BUT--

"JAVIER, WHY WOULD I BE HERE IF I ORDERED--"
"YOU WOULDN'T. YOU'D BE SILENT."

"ROTHSTEIN WAS INVISIBLE.
"NO ONE OTHER THAN THE HEADS OF HOUSES AND YOU--THE CHIEF OF THE MINUTE--

"GRAVES, YOU DIDN'T TELL YOUR MEN?"

"OF COURSE NOT."

"THEN THE HIT CAME FROM WITHIN THE TRUST."

"IT'S FUNNY...THE OLD GUARD IS DEAD. WHAT WE PLANNED HAS COME TO PASS...
"WHAT WE FORGOT TO PLAN FOR..."
...WAS THE NEW GUARD.
WHY I DIDN'T HAVE ANY CHILDREN, AUGUSTUS...?
"BECAUSE I WAS ONE, ONCE."
BAM-BA-BA-BA-BAM-BAM

BAM

NO, DIZZY... JESUS.

SO WHY DO YOU DO IT, WHY DO YOU TRY? ♪♪
♪ YOU GOT NO ANSWER, JUS' YER ITCHIN' TO FLY.
T'REE BUCKS? FUCK, I AIN'T PAID THAT LITTLE FER NO BEER IN...
I DON'T GOT POCKETS...
...
THAT'S GOTTA BE UP THERE AS THE LAMEST GODDAMN EXCUSE I EVER HEARD.

CHECK OUT THESE PANTS, WILEY. I AIN'T KIDDIN'.
GET ME NEXT TIME.
YOU GOT NO ANSWER, JUS' YER ITCHIN' TO FLY...
I ALWAYS DUG THIS BAND, BACK IN THE DAY.
HEARD THE SINGER WAS FUCKIN' DEAD THOUGH.
HE IS.
I GOTTA PISS.
GOOD LUCK WITH THAT.

BOREDOM IS THE REASON ♪
?
♪ BOREDOM IS THE REASON
YOU GOT NO FUCKIN' ZIPPER...
FUCK
BOREDOM IS THE REASON ♪
FUCK
FUCK
FUCK
BOREDOM IS THE REASON ♪

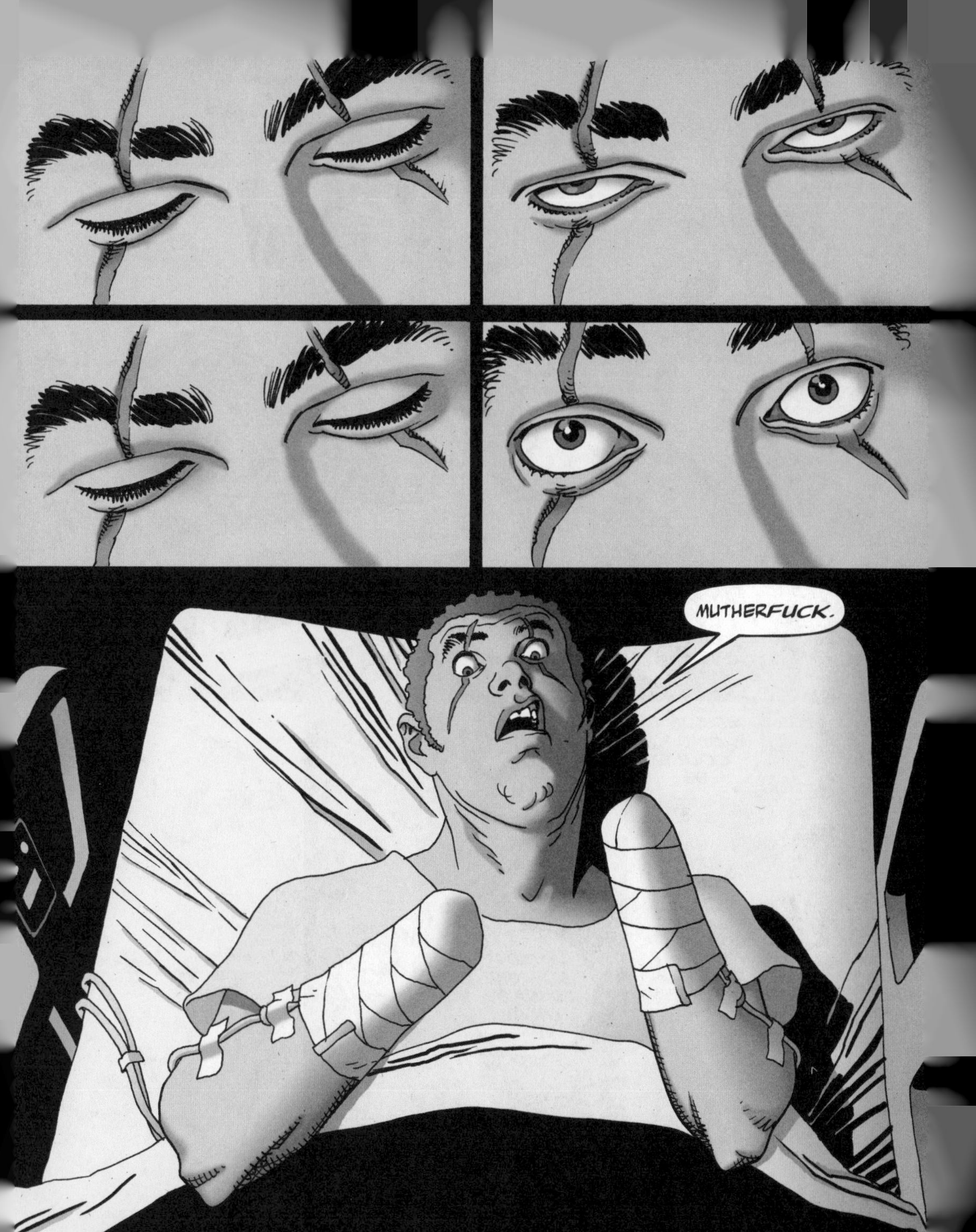

"100 BULLETS"

CHAPTER SEVEN: *DUCKS*

YER AWAKE...
I'M NOT HAPPY ABOUT IT.
WOULDN'T IMAGINE YOU COULD BE.
HOW LONG?
THREE DAYS.
DOCTOR SAYS YER GONNA BE OKAY, REMI.
YEAH? DO ME A FAVOR, VIC. WHEN DOCTOR BOOMBATZ COMES IN, CUT OFF HIS FUCKIN' HANDS SO'S I CAN TELL HIM HE'S OKAY TOO.
THIS IS, AH...
I KNOW. BAD DON' REALLY SUM IT UP.
NO, BAD RANKS PRETTY MUCH LIKE OKAY.

ial Hospital

I COULD USE SOME AIR.

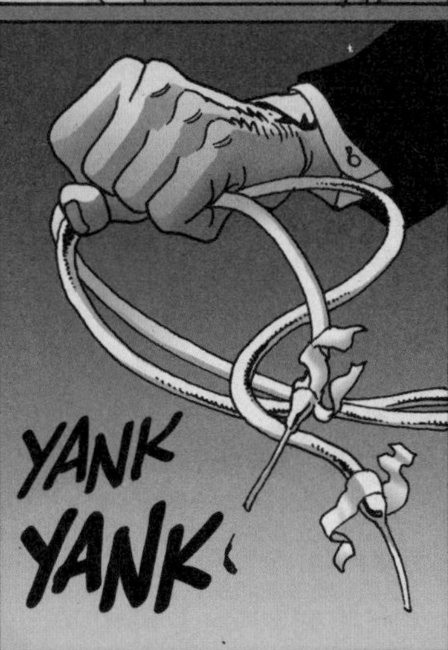

SO LET'S GET'CHA SOME.

YANK YANK

THERE'S ONE UP MY DICK, TOO, IF YOU DON' MIN'.
AH...
NAH...

DON' MIN' DRESSIN' YA, NEITHER.

WHERE TO?
AH... HANG ON...
TWO FIFTY-ONE EAST HURON.
NORTH-WESTERN?
YEAH, WHEREVER, ALL I GOT'S AN ADDRESS.
CLEAR CHANEL
FUNY CAB
1525
1525
TAXI
NO STOPPING
IT'S THE HOSPITAL--NORTHWESTERN.
251 E. HURON
OH FER CRYIN' OUT LOUD...
CHICAGO TAXI
SORRY, BUDDY. SOME-BODY--
MY BROTHER. I JUST CAME FROM A HOSPITAL TOO--IN CLEVELAND.
MY MOTHER.
I'M SORRY AGAIN.
27
SHE'S GONNA BE OKAY, JUST A LITTLE SCARE. ORIGINALLY THEY SAID WAS A FUCKIN' HEART ATTACK, BUT IT WAS JUS' THE AGITA.

KEPT HER IN, THOUGH.
WELL, THEY NEED TO MAKE SURE.
1525
A-135-C
50
11.23
SHE'S TOUGH, THAT OLD BROAD.
THAT'S GOOD. WHAT ABOUT YER BROTHER?
I GOT NO FUCKIN' CLUE.
JUST AN ADDRESS.
11.23
IT MIGHT NOT BE ANYTHING.
IT'S MY BROTHER...
EXIT 94
80
6
Chicago
EXIT 1/2 MILE
1525
A-135-C
SO AT LEAST IT'S A PAIN IN THE ASS.
"DAMN..."

...THESE THINGS'RE FUCKIN' STALE, VICTOR RAY.
C'MON, Y'KNOW I DON' SMOKE MUCH. THINK I BEEN CARRYIN' THESE SINCE WE WAS IN TAHOE.
NO WONDER IT TASTES DRY AS A MUMMY'S DICK.
HOW 'BOUT YOU GO GET A FRESH--
--REMI, WE'RE IN A GODDAMN HOSPITAL. I DON' THINK THEY SELL CIGARETTES IN THE GIFT SHOP HERE.
AN' YOU KNOW WHAT? THEY FUCKIN' SHOULD. OF ALL THE FUCKIN' PLACES...
AIN'T NOBODY HERE AIN'T DYIN' FER A SMOKE. EVEN THOSE THAT DON'T.
TOP IT OFF, PUT IN A BAR, FUCKIN' GOLD MINE. HAVE THIS PLACE PAYIN' FER ITSELF-- PUT THE INSURANCE COMPANIES OUT A' BUSINESS.

YOU MAY BE ON TO SOMETHIN' THERE...
FUCKIN' RIGHT I AM.

YOU, UM... WANNA GO TO A BAR?

ME? NAH. I'M ON MEDICATION, MIGHT GET AN ADVERSE REACTION.

SMOKIN' AN' DRINKIN'... WASN'T TALKIN' 'BOUT THE PATIENTS.
IF YOU WANNA GO GET A BOTTLE THOUGH...

I CAN WAIT.
"THIS TYPE OF SHIT IS TYPICAL OF MY BROTHER."

I MEAN, I GET A CALL--WHILE MY MA'S IN A FUCKIN' HOSPITAL BED--FROM SOME GUY I DON' KNOW SAYIN' MY BROTHER'S AT THIS ADDRESS AN' I NEED TO GO SEE 'IM.
I FIGURE HE'S FUCKIN' IN TROUBLE--'CAUSE HE ALWAYS FUCKIN' IS.
WELL, HE'S FAMILY.
THE SELFISH PRICK PLAYS ME LIKE A STRATO-CASTER.
IT'S MY FAULT, THOUGH. I SHOULDN'T FEEL RESPONSIBLE.
YOU CAN'T HELP IT.
1525

A PIECE OF SHIT.
HIM, BUT I CAN'T.
STILL, HE'S--
--YOUR BROTHER. YOU MUST LOVE HIM.
I KNOW. I WANT TO, BUT HE MAKES IT HARD, THE SHIT HE PULLS.
BUT YOU DO LOVE HIM.
YEAH, I DO. AT THE SAME TIME, I HATE HIM.
I HAD A CHANCE TO KILL HIM, ONCE.
DRIFTTTTT

SCREEECH

1525

WHUMP

FUCK YOU PIECE OF SHIT!

Y'OKAY?
THAT FUCKIN' ASSHOLE--HE'S GONNA CAUSE A **WRECK**.

I FUCKIN' **HATE** THOSE FUCKERS, THEY ACT LIKE THEY **OWN** THE ROAD.

THAT METER SAYS ***I'M*** THE ONE PAYIN' FOR IT NOW.

GO **AFTER** 'IM. GIVE 'IM A ***TASTE***.

"Y'KNOW, THE WAY YOU EXTRICATED YOURSELF FROM THAT ***WARZONE*** YOU CREATED?..."

I GOTTA HAND IT TO YOU.
"YOU TRYIN' TO BE A FUNNYMAN, VICTOR RAY?"
"WHA?--OH.
"POOR CHOICE A' WORDS."

WORDS SHMURDS...
...I'M TALKIN' BUSINESS HERE.
DID I GET THE FUCKIN' JOB DONE?
THE JOB... NO. YOU MANAGED TO WASTE EVERY-BODY BUT D'ARCY.

SHE FINGER ME?--HA!--NOW THAT'S FUNNY.

"SHE SPLIT TOWN. OMAHA."
"WHAT? UP TO VERMEER'S?"
"THAT MARONE... I COULD TAKE HIM OUT WITH ONE--
"--BOTH ARMS TIED BEHIND MY BACK."
"HOW 'BOUT YOU LET ME HANDLE IT, REMI?"
"SURE, SURE. WHY NOT...
"I MEAN, I'LL STAY HERE AN' LEARN HOW TO BEAT OFF WIT' A HOOK."

"I HEAR THERE ARE SOME GUYS...THEY, LIKE, DO IT WITH A *PILLOW.*"

"WHAT? *HOW* THE HELL?"

"THEY GET ON *TOP OF* IT..."

"THEY *FUCK A PILLOW?*"

"YEAH, MORE OR LESS."
"NO FUCKIN' *THANKS,* VIC. THAT IS FUCKIN' *TOO* GRIM."

"WHEN I WAS A KID, I HAD THIS FRIEND HAD THIS DOG. MAX HE WAS CALLED. SPENT HIS LIFE CHAINED IN THE BASEMENT."
A SPAZ POOCH. NOBODY LIKED 'IM. HE HAD A BLANKET, THOUGH, WHICH HE LIKED PLENTY.
WOULD HUMP THE SHIT OUT OF THAT THING.
SO MUCH, IT WOULD GET CRUSTY AN' STIFF, LIKE A TENT, 'TIL IT GOT WASHED, EVERY EIGHT MONTHS OR SO.
THE OTHER THING I REMEMBER ABOUT MAX WAS HIS EYES WERE ALWAYS WATERY.

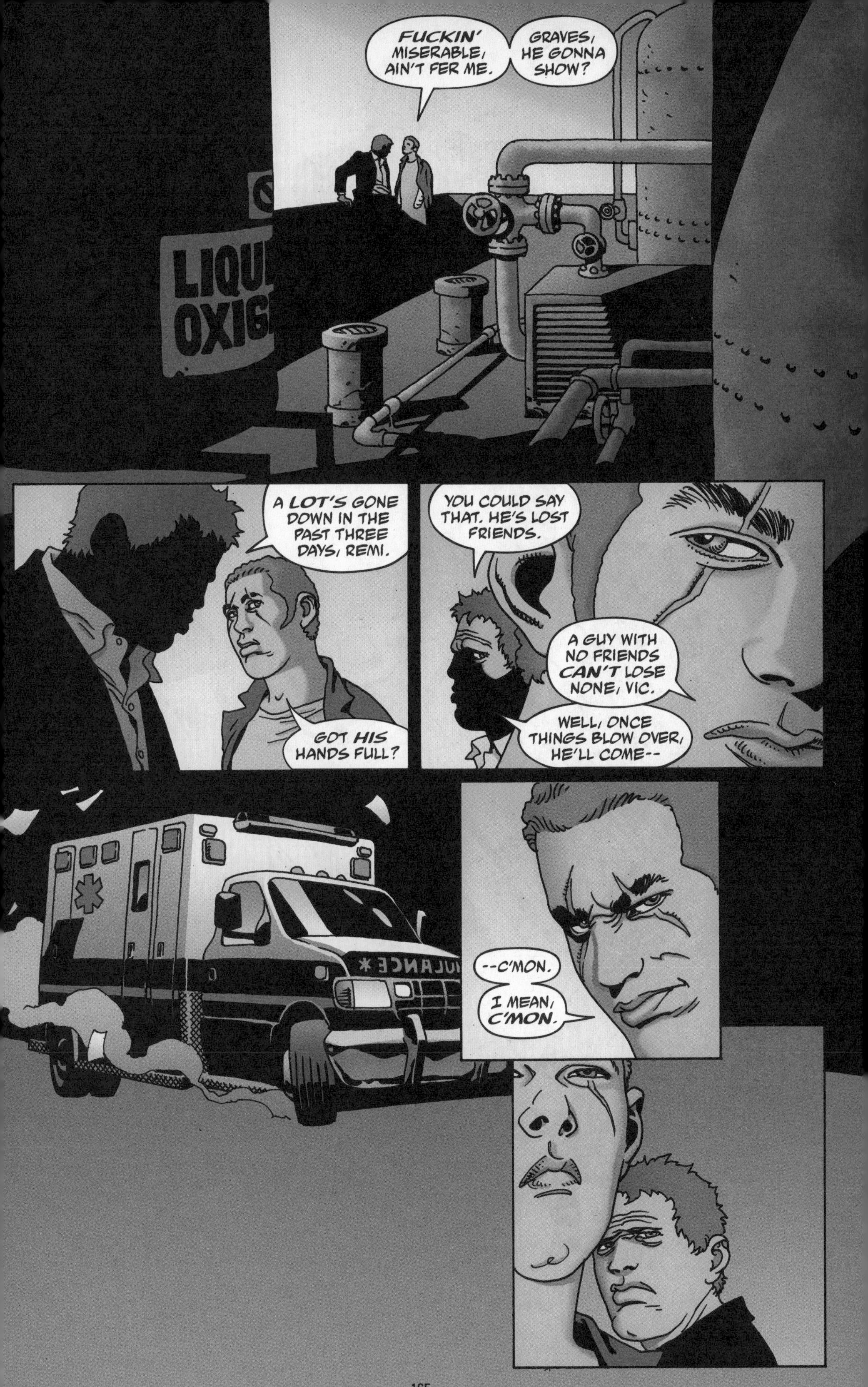

FUCKIN' MISERABLE, AIN'T FER ME.
GRAVES, HE GONNA SHOW?
LIQU
OXIG

A LOT'S GONE DOWN IN THE PAST THREE DAYS, REMI.
GOT HIS HANDS FULL?

YOU COULD SAY THAT. HE'S LOST FRIENDS.
A GUY WITH NO FRIENDS CAN'T LOSE NONE, VIC.
WELL, ONCE THINGS BLOW OVER, HE'LL COME--

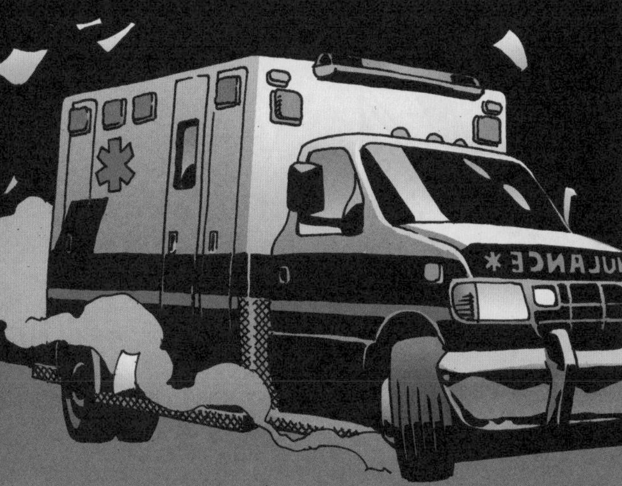

--C'MON.
I MEAN, C'MON.

YOU'LL BE TAKEN CARE OF.
THAT'S NOTHIN' I WANNA BE.
THERE ARE WORSE THINGS.
YER RIGHT...
JUS' LOOK AT THAT POOR FUCKIN' SUCK.
EVEN FROM UP HERE, TWENTY FUCKIN' STORIES--ALL I SEE IS RED. HE'S FUCKED.
BUT-- THESE FUCKIN' DOCTORS--FUCKIN' EGOMANIACS--ARE GONNA SAVE HIS FUCKIN' LIFE.
EMS

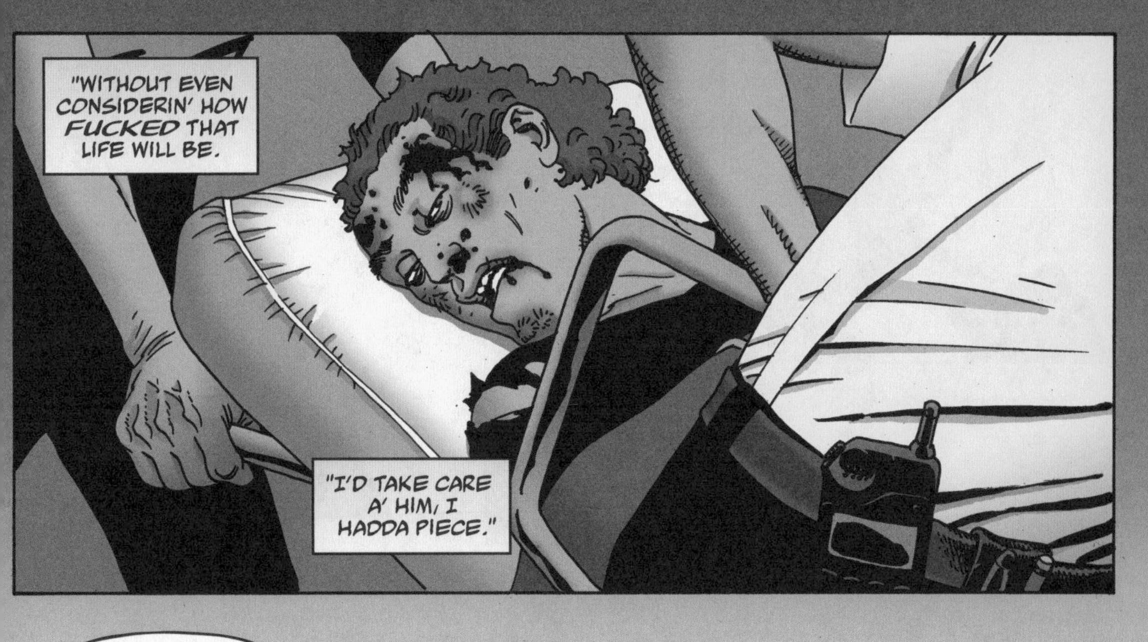
"WITHOUT EVEN CONSIDERIN' HOW FUCKED THAT LIFE WILL BE.
"I'D TAKE CARE A' HIM, I HADDA PIECE."

YOU COULD HIT ANYTHING, AT ABOUT ANY DISTANCE, I'LL GIVE YOU THAT.
ANYTHING.

WASN'T A BETTER SHOT IN THE CREW.

I DON' KNOW. WYLIE HAD SICK AIM.
FUCK THAT GUY.

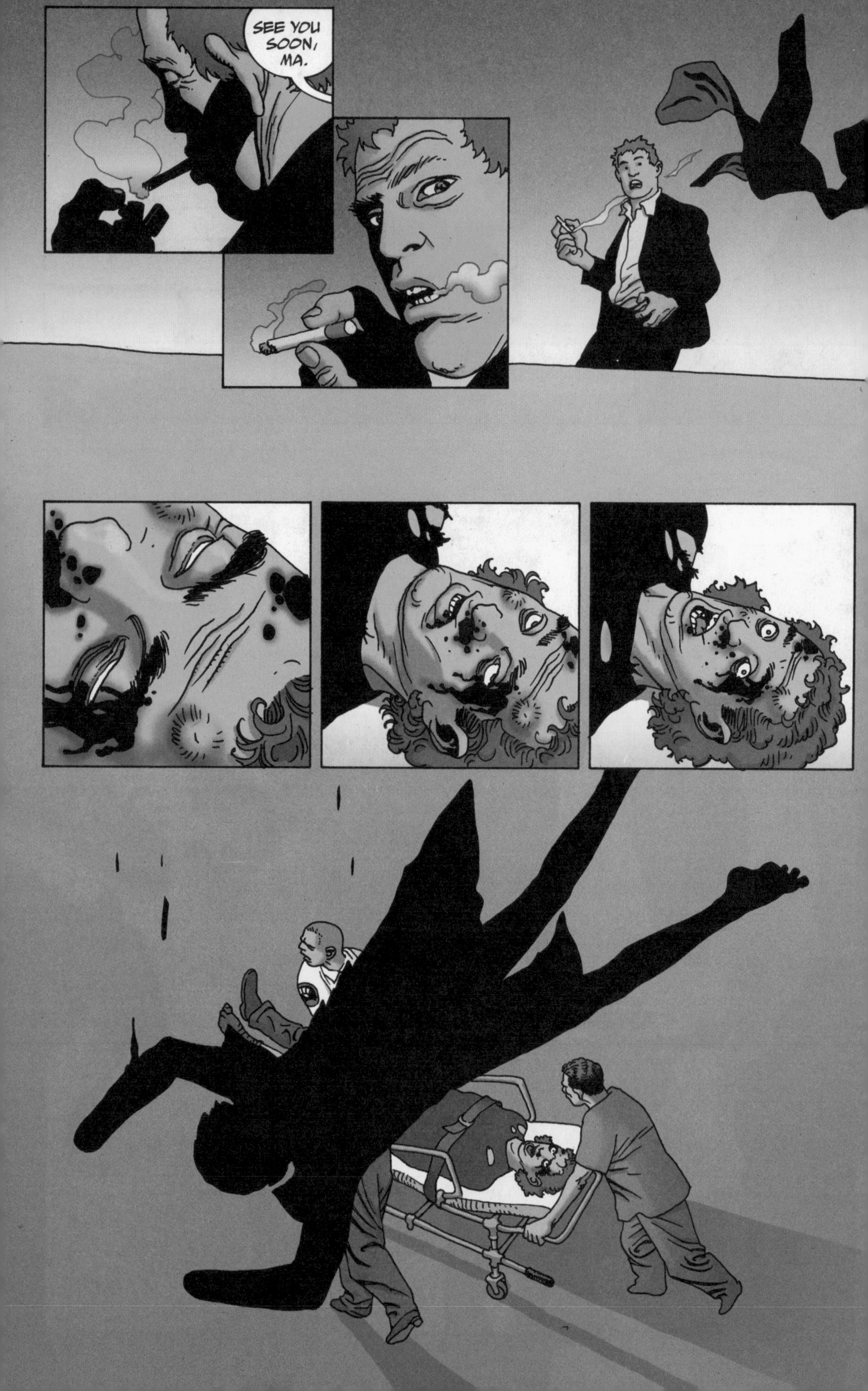

SEE YOU SOON, MA.

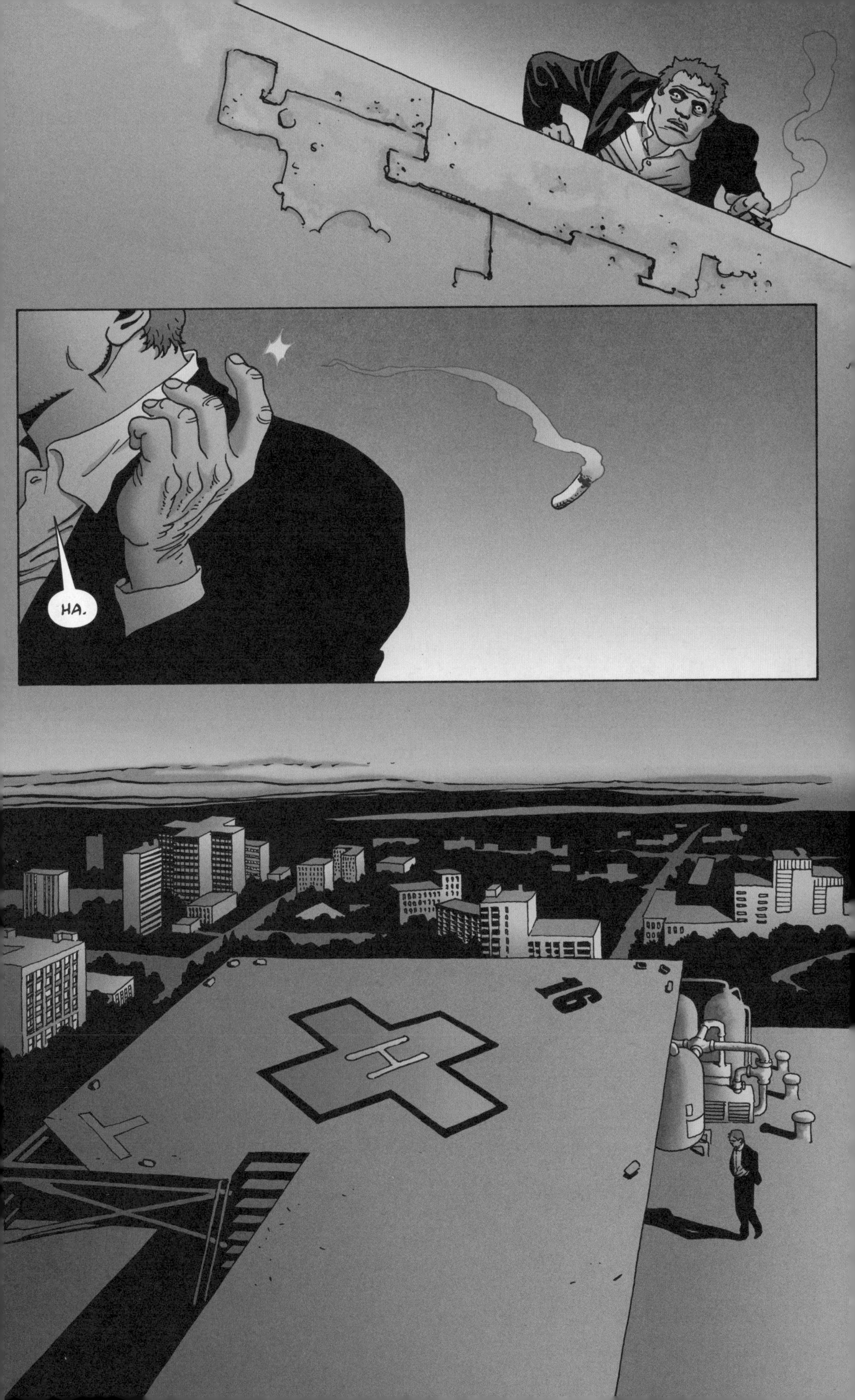

HA.
16
H

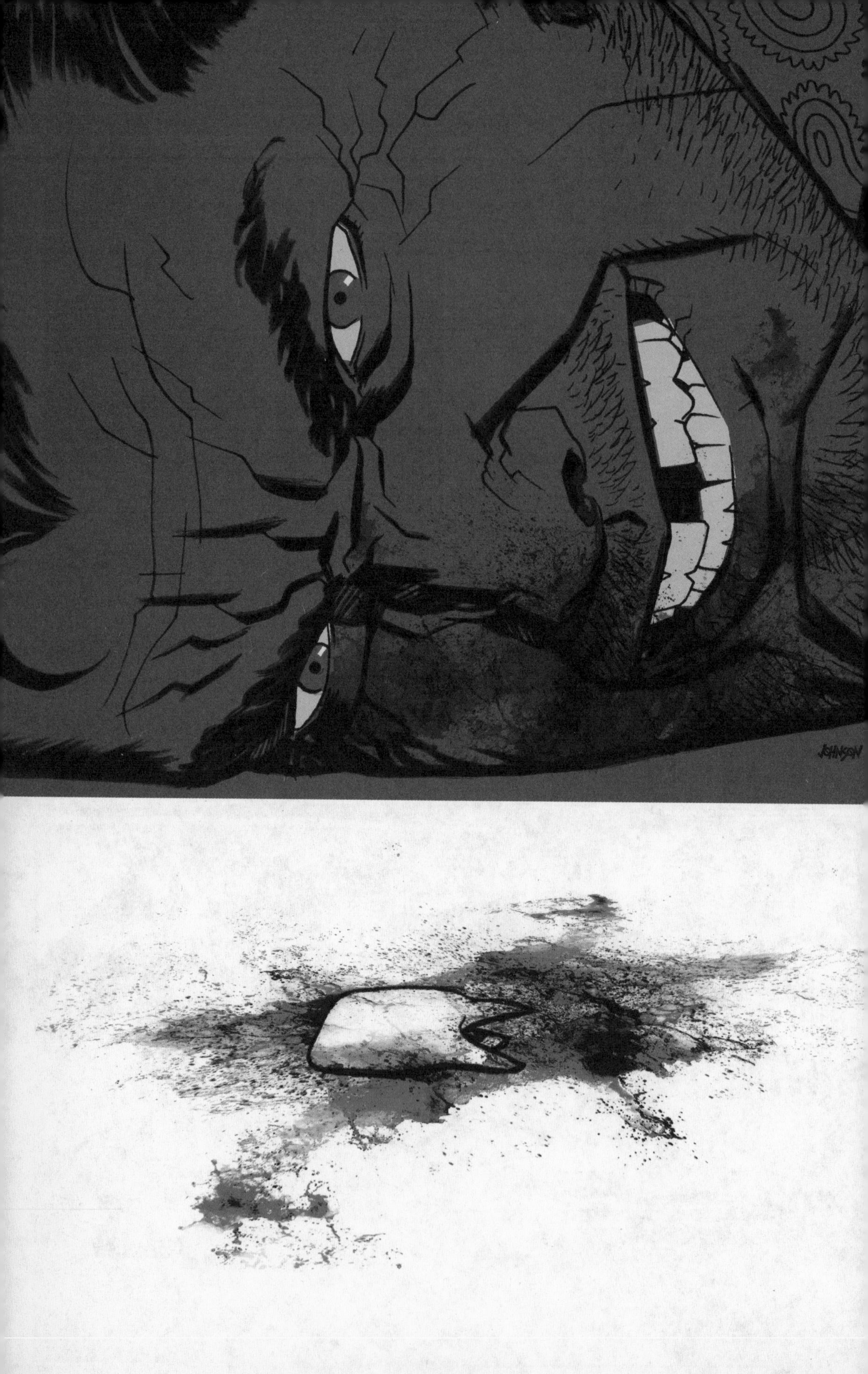

LONO
BD-RING BD-RING
HELLO, LONO.
WHAT'S UP, BENNY?
SEEMS A WILD HAIR IN EVERY ASS.
WHY THANK YOU, THANK YOU VERY MUCH.
YOU LIKE THAT, DON'T YOU?-- CAUSING TROUBLE.
LIKE? NAH... CAN'T SEEM TO NOT, THOUGH. WHY YOU THINK THAT IS?
DON'T ASK ME TO TRY AN' FIGURE YOU OUT.
WHERE YOU BEEN?
ON THE ROAD. GOIN' ON FOUR DAYS, AN' JUST AS MANY CARS...

95 South Miami

Miami Int'l Airport

1

East to 95 South Downtown

...GOT A **PRESENT** FOR YOU...

BD-RING
DIZZY
BD-RING
WHATEVER YOU'VE DONE TO *HER*, I WILL DO TO *YOU*.
OOH... BE *STILL*, MY BEATING HEART...
I'LL MAKE *THAT* HAPPEN *TOO*, LONO.
C'MON, GRAVES, RECOGNIZE A LITTLE *GAME* HERE.

"YOU TOOK OUT A BUNCH OF PIKERS. I'M S'POSED TO BE *IMPRESSED?...*

"I KNOW WHAT TO *EXPECT* FROM YOU, LONO.

"AND FOR THAT MATTER, WHAT *NOT* TO.

"YOU *MIGHT* HAVE IMPRESSED ME IF YOU DIDN'T LEAVE YOUR 'MASTER' BEHIND...

"...WITH *ME."*

"GRAVES, I HAD NO IDEA YOU WERE ON THE PREMISES, 'TIL THE *SHIT* WAS ON ITS WAY TO THE FAN. BY THEN, I DIDN'T *GIVE* A RAT'S ASS...

"SO AUGUSTUS, HE *DEAD?*"

"NOT YET. IS...

"...DIZZY?"

"YOU LOOKING TO *TRADE?* SHOVE IT UP YER *PIE-HOLE.*

"AS FOR AUGUSTUS?
"DO IT, GRAVES...
"I DARE YOU."
"CONSIDER IT DONE, LONO. IF FOR NO OTHER REASON THAN TO PUT YOU OUT OF WORK."
"FAT CHANCE OF THAT, DICKWEED."
"REALLY? THE HEADS OF THE REMAINING HOUSES MAY BE SCARED OF YOU, BUT THEY'RE NOT STUPID. AUGUSTUS IS YOUR ONLY ADVOCATE IN THE TRUST."

TRUE...

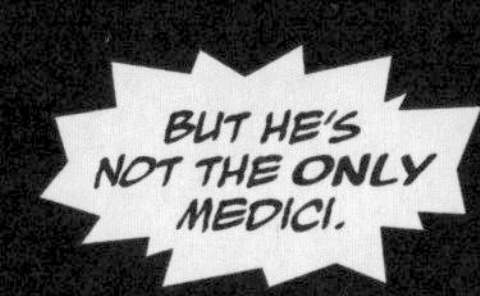
BUT HE'S NOT THE ONLY MEDICI.

BD-RING

HEY, I GOT ANOTHER CALL I GOTTA TAKE.
CLIC

LOOP? WHERE THE FUCK YOU--
--NO, FUCK YOU...

...SHIT.
YEP.
YOU KILL IM?
I'M ALIVE. DO THE MATH.
GODDAMNIT. JACK?
ONE...MINUS THREE, EQUALS--?
?
THREE?
NO, DUMBASS...
IT EQUALS YER NEXT.

HEH.
CLIC
WHAT YOU DO THAT FOR?
I JUS' WANTED TO FUCK WIT' 'IM.
LIKE I WAS FUCKIN' WITH YOU.
SMILE
"LOOK, LOOP...
"...WHEN I CAME TO...
"...I WENT LOOKIN' FOR YOU. I PULLED YOU UP FROM THAT FUCKIN' DITCH, DIDN' I?
"TAKIN' YOU OUT TO THE WOODS, WAS JUST HAVIN' SOME FUN."

I NEVER HAD NO INTENTION OF **KILLIN'** YOU.
WELL, *I* DID OF **YOU**.
KID, YOU GOTTA LIGHTEN **UP**.
ANYWHO, LONO TOL' ME WHAT I WANTED TO KNOW. JACK AIN'T BEEN IN CONTACT WIT' 'IM.
MEANIN'?
THAT'S WHAT I **DON'** KNOW. HE COULD BE WITH GRAVES, BUT I'M GONNA DO SOMETHIN' **NOBODY** DOES FER HIJACK...
GIVE HIM SOME CREDIT?
YOU AN' I, WE'RE HAVIN' THIS CONVERSATION 'CAUSE HE'S **ALLOWED** US TO...

"...DON' WORRY ABOUT THE HAWAIIAN. I'LL CALL 'IM BACK IN A FEW HOURS, SETTLE HIS NERVES."
HOW'D YOUR OTHER CALL GO, LONO?
WHY DON'T YOU TELL ME?

...

FROM YOUR TONE, IT WENT WELL...
...FOR ONE OF US.

YEAH...YEAH, IT DID. BUT I'LL TELL YOU SOMETHIN'--AN' YOU CAN TELL THAT SHIT--I WILL HUNT HIM DOWN, PULL HIS HEAD OUT OF YER ASS, AN' SAW IT OFF WITH MY FINGERNAILS.
EASY, BOY...

WHAT THE FUCK KINDA...?
I'LL PULL COLE'S COCK OFF TOO AN' CHOKE YOU WITH IT, YOU TALK TO ME LIKE THAT!

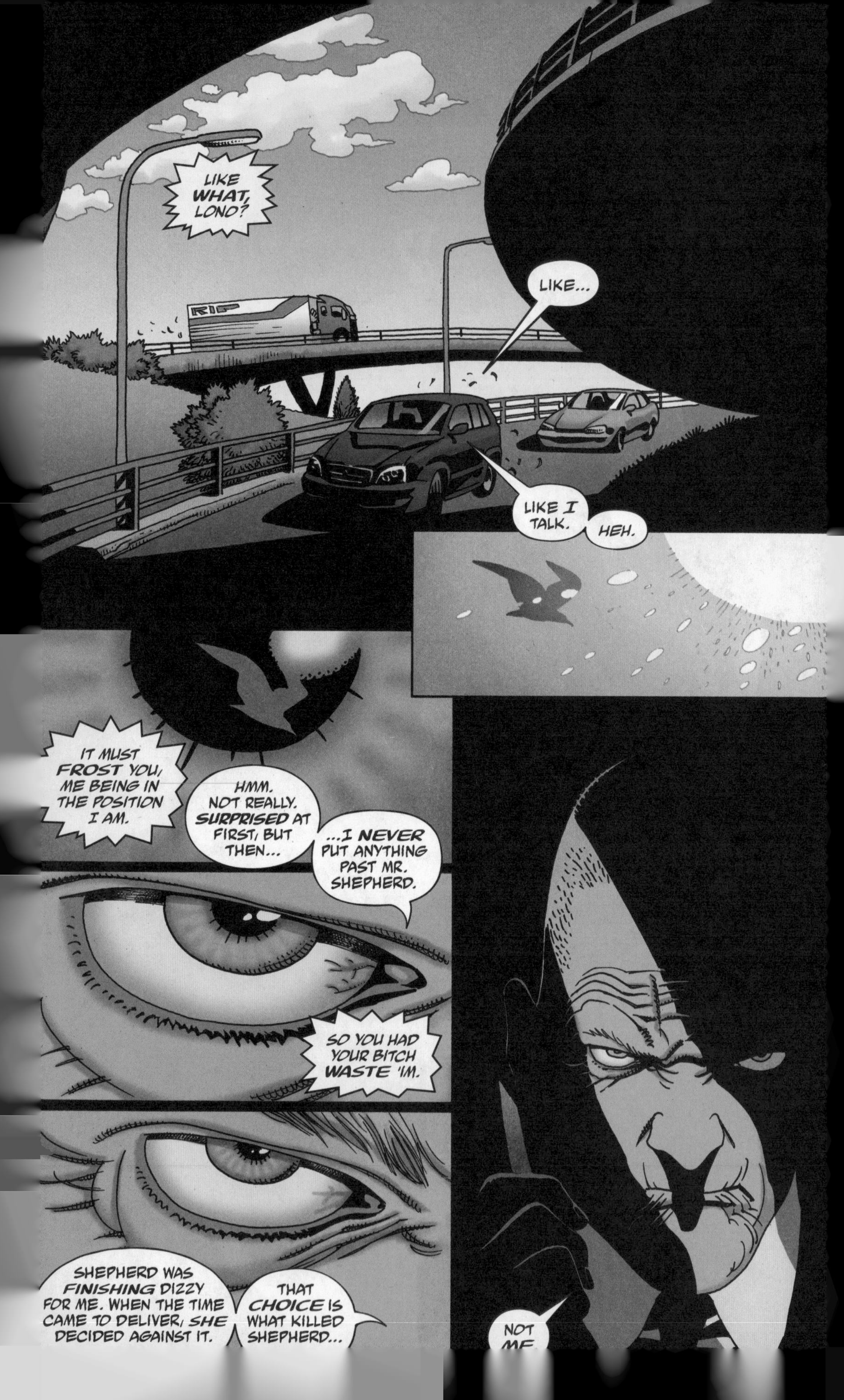
LIKE WHAT, LONO?
LIKE...
LIKE I TALK.
HEH.
IT MUST FROST YOU, ME BEING IN THE POSITION I AM.
HMM. NOT REALLY. SURPRISED AT FIRST, BUT THEN...
...I NEVER PUT ANYTHING PAST MR. SHEPHERD.
SO YOU HAD YOUR BITCH WASTE 'IM.
SHEPHERD WAS FINISHING DIZZY FOR ME. WHEN THE TIME CAME TO DELIVER, SHE DECIDED AGAINST IT.
THAT CHOICE IS WHAT KILLED SHEPHERD...
NOT ME.

HAHAHA... WHAT'S IT LIKE-- HAVIN' A BULL'S ASSHOLE FOR A MOUTH?

IT'S NO EXCUSE, LONO. I'M DEAD SERIOUS.
LIFE IS ALL ABOUT CHOICES-- ACTIVELY MAKING THEM.
YOU READ MUCH?

WHAT?
I ASKED YOU IF YOU READ-- NOT THAT I CARE. MY POINT IS...
WHEN I WAS YOUNGER, I STARTED READING A BOOK. IT WAS CALLED THE BOOK OF SHOULD...

AS IN, EACH CHAPTER... YOU SHOULD GO TO COLLEGE, YOU SHOULD GET A JOB, YOU SHOULD FALL IN LOVE...
BUY A HOUSE, GET MARRIED, HAVE CHILDREN...

I GOT BORED WITH IT, BECAUSE I KNEW HOW IT WAS GOING TO END.

I LEFT THAT BOOK ON A TRAIN A LONG TIME AGO.
DIZZY REACTED TO A WORD--
CROATOA--
--YES. IT WAS A FAIL-SAFE. IF SHE HEARD IT FROM ME, SHEPHERD WOULD STILL BE ALIVE.
THAT SHE DIDN'T WAS NOT MY CHOICE.
YER THE WORST KIND OF LIAR, GRAVES...
THE KIND THAT LIES TO HIMSELF.
YOU AIN'T WHAT YOU THINK YOU ARE.
WHO IS, LONO? ARE YOU?
I AM VERY COMFORTABLE IN MY SKIN.
REALLY? WHAT IF I TOLD YOU I HAD A FAIL-SAFE WORD FOR YOU...
ONE THAT WOULD CALM YOU DOWN A BIT...

NO, SAY A **LOT**. ONE THAT WOULD TAKE THE EDGE OFF. THAT EDGE YOU **LIVE** OFF OF.
ONE THAT WOULD MAKE YOU THINK **TWICE**, TURN THOSE BRASS BALLS OF YOURS TO **SOUR GRAPES**.
IF YOU DID, YOU'D **USE** IT.
WHAT IF I JUST **DID**?
WHAT ARE YOU SAYING!?
GIVE ME THE GIRL BACK.
CASINO
Atlantic

...
END CALL
FUCK.
FUCKFUCK
FUCKFUCK
FUCK--
MOTHER FUCKER!

YOU LOOK HAPPY WITH YOURSELF.
HAPPY? NO, JAVIER. BUT I MAY HAVE SOLVED A PROBLEM.
HOW?
BY CREATING ANOTHER ONE.
GRAVES--
PHIL?
...
IT'S JUST MY OPINION...

...BUT NO, AUGUSTUS...
LONO ISN'T CAPABLE OF FINESSE.
WHAT HE SAYS, HE SAYS 'CAUSE IT'S ACTUAL.
I'M SORRY.

THE MEETING IN OMAHA-- IS HE THERE?
NO...

"...HE'S IN MIAMI."
JESUS... ARE YOU ALL RIGHT?

WHAT?

YOUR FACE.

OH.
DON'T ASK, JUST ACCEPT.
FUCKING TRIBUTE. THIS...

...AND THAT.

YOUR *MINUTEMAN,* BENITO.
LIVE OR DEAD?
TAKE A *LOOK.*

I CAN *MAKE* YOU GET OUT OF MY WAY.
NO, PIN-DICK, YOU *CAN'T.*
AND IF YOU *TRY--*
YOU WILL DIE.
BECAUSE THAT IS WHAT YOU MINUTEMEN *DO.*
IS THAT WHY YOU DIDN'T--

"NO, LONO. WHEN I WAS ASKED TO JOIN THE MINUTEMEN...
"I THINK...I UNDERSTOOD WHAT GUARDING THE CASTLE MEANT.
"THE STEPS SEEMED SAFER.
"BUT THAT'S SOMETHING ONLY LIONS KNOW."
SO, BENNY--

BAAAM

"100 BULLETS"

CHAPTER EIGHT:
DAMAGED GOOD

"I DON'T BELIEVE THINGS COULD BE ANY MORE BROKEN THAN THEY ARE.

"THE TRUST IS IN *PIECES*.
"NO ONE'S WORD MEANS ANYTHING...

"MINE *INCLUDED*, OF COURSE."

"GRAVES AND WHAT'S LEFT OF HIS MINUTEMEN ARE EVEN MORE FRACTURED.
70

"IT'S ESSENTIAL FOR THEM TO BE ABLE TO RELY ON EACH OTHER--AND THAT'S GONE.

IT'S REALLY UNNERVING HOW UNRECOGNIZABLE OUR WORLD'S BECOME...

TRULY UNNERVING...

AND I WOULDN'T HAVE IT *ANY* OTHER WAY.

"100 BULLETS"

CHAPTER NINE FEARSOMALITY CRISIS

SO NOW WHAT?
NOW, JOAN, WE GET A SIT-DOWN.
ON OUR TERMS.
DO YOU THINK THAT'S A POSSIBILITY, TIBO?
IT HAS TO BE. OR WE REFUSE.
"LOOK, I THINK WE CAN ALL ADMIT, WHEN GRAVES STARTED TO CUT OFF THE HEADS...
"...WE WERE MORE THAN HAPPY TO ABSORB THE HOUSES INTO OUR OWN."
GREED IS A HELL OF A MOTIVATOR.
GREED AND GRAVES.
HA...BUT IT WAS AUGUSTUS' PLAN.
AND IT WASN'T A HARD SELL.

GREED AND FEAR.
BUT **NO** HOUSE HAD THE INFRASTRUCTURE TO TAKE ON A PIECE OF ANOTHER--
LET ALONE ***EIGHT.*** WE GOT ***RICHER,*** SAME TIME? WE GOT ***WEAKER.***
NOT ***EVERY*** HOUSE.
NO, TIBO...VASCO AND MEDICI WERE PREPARED. NONE OF THE ***REST*** OF US WERE, THOUGH.
THAT WAS BY ***DESIGN.***
WHAT ABOUT BENITO? IF THINGS GET ***MESSY...***
I HOPE HE'LL RECOGNIZE AN ***OPPORTUNITY.***

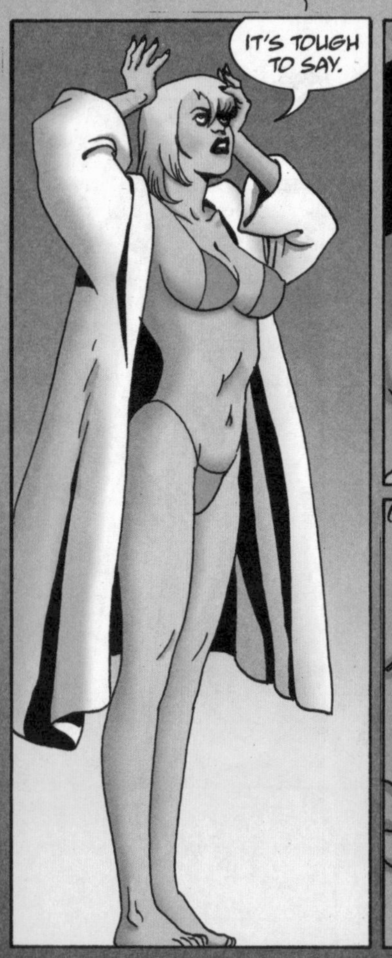

DO YOU HAVE ***ANY*** SWAY OVER HIM OR ***NOT?***

"I DO."

WHAT THE FUCK?

YOU'RE GIVING HIM *COVER.* I CAN'T HEAR HIM MOVE.

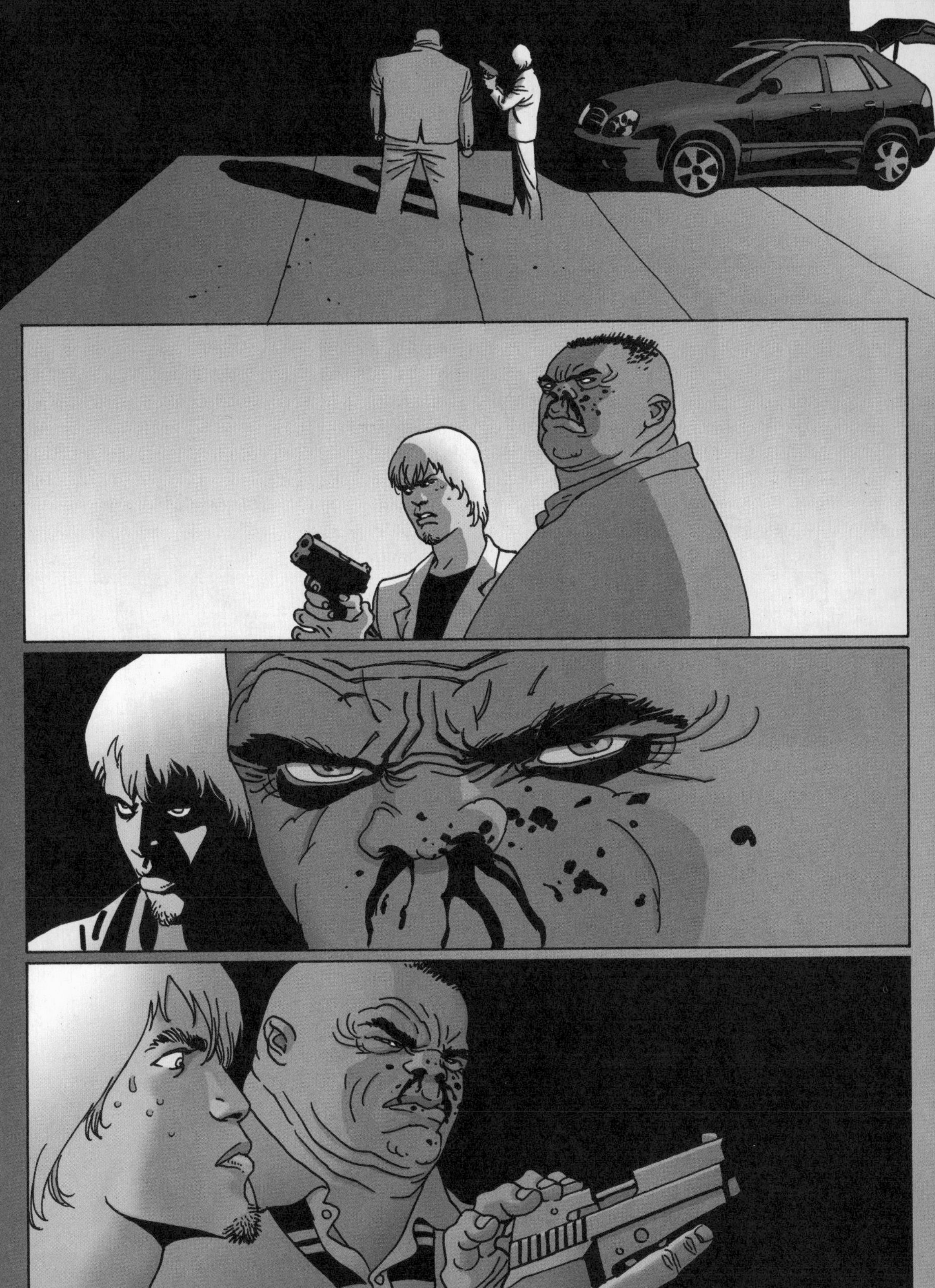

GET THE GIRL.
BRING HER INSIDE.

HE'S GONE.

ATTENTION, ALL POSTS...

CODE SEVEN...

SECURE THE PREMISES.

"IT'S TIME TO *END* THIS WAR..."

...IT'S OVER.
ARE YOU OUT OF YOUR MIND, AUGUSTUS?
PHIL...
"THE GRAND PLAN, I'M TAKING IT OFF THE TABLE. WE SETTLE WITH WHAT WE'VE GAINED, AND--"
WE? WHAT IN THE HELL HAVE I GAINED?
PERHAPS MORE THAN THE TRUST. THE MINUTEMEN WILL BE REINSTATED.
YOU'LL HOLD A DISTINCT ADVANTAGE OVER FIVE HOUSES.
I WAS NEVER INTERESTED IN AN ADVANTAGE. YOU WANT TO QUIT? FINE.
...I HAVE WORK TO DO.

AM I THE ONLY ONE WHO'S THINKING CLEARLY HERE?
NOW IS NOT THE TIME TO GO SOFT.
JAVIER...
...YOU HAVE NO IDEA WHAT TIME IT IS.
REALLY? GRAVES, HOW MANY MEN HAVE YOU AT THIS MINUTE?
"I'LL TAKE THAT SILENCE TO MEAN LESS THAN YOU'RE COMFORTABLE WITH.
"SEEING THIS THROUGH WILL MEAN LESS THAN YOU CAN LIVE WITH.
"AND AUGUSTUS, GIVING THE MINUTEMEN THE UPPER HAND IS SUICIDE."
WHAT DO YOU SUGGEST, JAVIER?
LISTENING. WE CALL OMAHA...

"...ONLY AFTER WE AGREE HOW THIS IS GOING TO END."
BENITO, HE'S GROWN--
"I'VE HELPED HIM, IN SOME WAYS.
"AT THE SAME TIME THOUGH, I WONDER, IF WHAT HE DOES IS MAINLY FOR HIS FATHER'S APPROVAL."
YOU WONDER--
SHOULD WE BE CONCERNED?

WE SHOULD BE AWARE, TIBO.
IF THINGS GET GRIM, I CAN'T PROMISE YOU WHICH SIDE HE'LL TAKE.
WELL, THERE'S TWO SIDES TO EVERY BRIDGE.
WE'LL CROSS THAT ONE WHEN WE GET THERE.
AND HOW DO WE GET THERE?
TAKING THE MORAL HIGH ROAD.
"TAKING? WE ALREADY HAVE IT."
WE AREN'T THE CRIMINALS HERE. TWO HOUSES UNITED AND MOVED AGAINST EVERY OTHER HOUSE IN THE TRUST.
HEADS ARE DEAD--MY FATHER FOR ONE--BRUTALLY MURDERED.
AND THERE WAS A TIME THERE WERE MEN TO DEAL WITH THAT SORT OF THING.
NOW, THERE ARE MURDERERS.

...WE MAKE A DEAL WITH THEM.

YOU MEAN WITH *GRAVES?*

"NO, I SAID WITH *THEM.*

"GIVEN THE STATE OF THE *WORLD...*

"...I THINK THEY'LL *LISTEN.*"
HUH. HE AIN'T ANSWERIN'.
BD-RNG

FLORIDA WELCOMES YOU
INTERSTATE
SOME SURPRISE. YOU FUCKIN' TOL' HIM YOU WAS GONNA WASTE 'IM.
SO HE'S SCARED.
YEAH, COLE, THAT'S WHAT HE IS--LIKE KING MUTHAFUCKIN' KONG WAS A' PLANES.
THAT WAS SOME STOOPID SHIT, PISSIN' LONO OFF.
THOSE PLANES...
...KILLED THE BIG APE.
HEY!
"WHY THE HELL YOU INVOLVED IN ALL THIS, LOOP?...
"YOU DON' HAVE TO BE."
...
MY FATHER...

WAS A GOOD MAN. WE ALL RESPECTED HIM.
TRUTH, HE SHOULD HAVE BEEN ONE OF US, IF NOT FOR...
OKAY, I SMELL YEA.
NO YOU DON', AN' DON' PRETEND TO. I GOT THE ATTACHÉ FROM GRAVES, AN' MY POP'S PICTURE WAS IN IT.
I WAS TOL' THE MAN Y'ALL RESPECT-- SUPPOSABLY FUCKIN' WRECKED MY LIFE.
MAYBE I HATE ON THE FACT THAT Y'ALL KNEW 'IM BETTER THAN I DID.

KNOCK KNOCK

"FOLLOWIN' IN YER OLD MAN'S FOOTSTEPS--IS PROBABLY SOMETHING HE'D KICK YER **ASS** FOR DOING.

"LOOP, LOOK--THIS LIFE--THIS FUCKIN' LIFE...IT ENDS **ONE** WAY."

"EVERYONE'S DOES, COLE--THE SAME WAY.

"MIGHT AS WELL BE **FUCKIN'** WHEN IT DOES.

"AND SPEAKIN' A KONG, WEREN'T NO **PLANES** DID 'IM. EVERYBODY KNOWS..."

"...WAS BEAUTY KILLED THE BEAST."
"SO ARE WE IN AGREEMENT?..."

I'M NOT GOING TO AGREE, JAVIER. BUT I WON'T DISAGREE EITHER.
PHIL?

WHAT YOU'RE ASKING ME TO DO...
--NOT TO DO. I KNOW...

IT RUBS YOU THE WRONG WAY, TIBO?
WE HAVE TO MAKE THEM UNDERSTAND WE'RE PREPARED FOR THINGS TO GET WORSE...

...BEFORE THEY GET BETTER.

NOW IS THE TIME TO FORCE WHAT THEY *THINK* IS THE SOLUTION...

...DOWN THEIR *THROATS*.

I'M NOT COMFORTABLE WITH IT. FROM A *NUMBERS* STANDPOINT.

THE DECIDING VOTE IS *IMPORTANT*. IF WE DO THIS, IT'LL BE OURS.
ASSUMING *WE* ARE ON THE SAME PAGE.

ASSUMING THEY'LL SIT *DOWN*.
THEY *WILL*. IN FACT, THEY'LL COME TO US *ASKING* FOR IT.

WE HAVE TO END THE TURMOIL AND PUT THE TRUST BACK TOGETHER. AND IF IT HAS NO RESEMBLANCE TO WHAT IT WAS...

THEY'LL HAVE NO IDEA WHAT WE THREE CAN MAKE IT BE.

FOR THAT TO HAPPEN, DO WE REALLY NEED ANOTHER DEATH?

I THINK THIS IS THE WAY TO GO.

ONE MORE...
AND IT'S OVER.

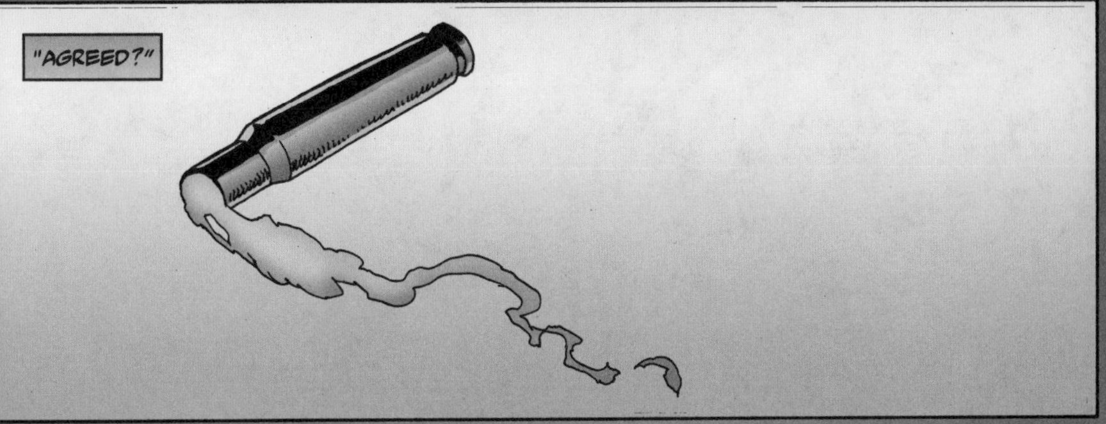
"AGREED?"

TINK

XIII
JOHNSON

HELLO?
HELLO, HOW ARE YOU?
STILL ALIVE. YOU?
GRAVES
7:12

THE SAME. I GUESS THE TWO OF US, WE MADE IT OUT. NOT THAT I HAD ANY DOUBT WE WOULD.
MADE IT OUT?
I WAS ON THE TRIGGER...

AND I GOT CALLED OFF.

SEEMS THE TRUST AN' THE MINUTEMEN DONE KISSED AN' MADE UP.
WHAT? THAT DON' MAKE SENSE...

SOMETHIN' IN THE MILK AIN'T CLEAN.

YOU PROLLY AIN'T THE ONLY ONE THAT FEELS THAT WAY. I BEEN CHARGED TO DEAL WITH THE ONES THAT DO.
AN' I AIN'T SAYIN' I LIKE THAT, NEITHER. BUT LIFE AIN'T EVER BEEN ABOUT LIKIN' NOTHIN'.

WHICH, I ADMIT, I CAN LIVE WITH.

HAVE YOU BEEN IN TOUCH WITH GRAVES? I KNOW HE'S CONCERNED--

"100 BULLETS"

CHAPTER TEN: FIVE ROOK(ED)S

HOW WAS OMAHA, MEGAN?
DULL, BENITO...
COMPARATIVELY.
IS AUGUSTUS BACK YET?
ON HIS WAY.
WITH GRAVES.
AND THE REST OF THE TRUST?
FOLLOWING ME.

HEH.
I GOT TO ADMIT, YOU ARE FOXY...
IS THAT A COMPLIMENT I SHOULD FIND OFFENSIVE?
YOU WANT TO GET POLITICALLY CORRECT?...
THE MEETING TONIGHT, THE SETTLEMENT... BIG MISTAKE.
WELL, YOU SHOULD SAVE YOUR OPINION FOR EVERYONE THERE.
I WOULD, BUT I WON'T BE.
DADDY'S ORDERS. IT'S JUST THE FIVE OF YOU...
SHAKING HANDS, AND BURYING DIFFERENCES ON TOP OF THE BODIES THAT FOUGHT FOR THEM.

MIAMI HERALD
Picante
SHOULDN' PUT THAT ON EVERYTHIN', COLE. ALL THEM PEPPERS?...
SANDMAN
MOTEL
SINGLE $15
FREE CABLE TV
FOR RENT
ENTRA
DINNER
El POLLO LOCO
BAR-B-Q
YOU TRYIN' TO SHIT OUT YER ASSHOLE?
YEAH. LIKE EVERYBODY ELSE.
SO WE HERE NOW. READY TO TELL ME WHY?
SURE. TO SEE YER BOSS.
NO, NOT LONO. HIS BOSS. THE BOSS.
YOU BEEN OUT TO MEDICI'S?
POLLO LOCO

NAH. LONO... HE KEPT ME AN' JACK AWAY. SAID ONE FACE WAS BEST.
CAN'T ARGUE WITH THAT.
POLLO LOCO
HIS BOY, THOUGH--HE WAS AWARE OF US.
MIAMY HE
TSUNAMI
LEAVE MORE THAN THOUSAND DEATH

BENITO? WHAT'S YER READ ON HIM?
HE'S, AH... LONO--

--PUSHED HIM AROUND?
--USED THE WORDS HE'D LISTEN TO, KNOWHUMSAYIN'?

RIGHT.
AIN'T ENOUGH...
I GOTTA GO GET MORE.

DAMN... YOU ARE LOOKIN' TO DIE IN THE WORST WAY.
I AIN'T LOOKIN' FOR--
FUCK.
LOOP...
POLLO LOCO

THAS' OUR RIDE.

JACK...
YOU GOTTA BE SHITTIN' ME-- A FUCKIN' COINCIDENCE?

MEANS THIS IS GONE BAD.
WHAT? WE FUCKIN' LUCKY...
AIN'T NO SUCH THING-- LIKE HOPE.
FUCKIN' COINCIDENCE. GODDAMMIT...
LIKE THERE IS A FUCKIN' GOD...
DINER
El POLLO LOCO
BAR-B-Q

SOMETHING PREYING ON YOUR *MIND,* AUGUSTUS?

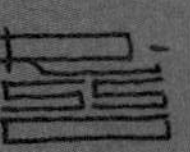

EXCUSE ME?
YOU LOOK DISTRACTED.

SO I'M A *MIRROR,* PHIL?

YOU *BLAME* ME? THIS ISN'T EXACTLY *NEUTRAL GROUND* WE'RE TREADING ON.

NO...BUT THERE ISN'T ANY OF THAT *LEFT.*

I'VE BEEN ROLLING IT OVER IN MY MIND, WHY JAVIER WAS THEIR TARGET...
"OUT OF US THREE, HE MADE THE LEAST SENSE. IN MANY RESPECTS, HE WAS AN ALLY-- ONE THEY MAY HAVE NEEDED. BUT...
"...I SEE THE IMPORTANCE OF HAVING ME BROKERING THE TREATY.
"SURE, THERE'S A BIT OF EGG--AT THE SAME TIME IT SAVES MY FACE..."
AND THEIRS, TOO.
"AND IF IT WAS YOU, PHIL, WHO WAS ASSASSINATED...
"...WELL, WHO KNOWS HOW THE REMAINING MINUTEMEN WOULD REACT?

YOU, WE HAVE THEM.
OR SO THE THEORY GOES. BUT I DO AGREE...
VICTOR RAY
"...ALL IN ALL, WELL PLAYED."

GODDAMMIT...
BAAM

GIMME A REASON...
KEEPING A PROMISE.
TO A GUY I GOT KINDA CLOSE WITH...A LITTLE GUY...WITH A LOT OF FUCKIN' HEART.
YOU GOT ONE?
NOT THE KIND A' PERSON YOU'D KNOW, JACK...

STOMACH.
COLE, I LEFT YOU ALIVE...
...'CAUSE I LOST THE APPETITE FOR KILLIN'.
IT'S A ROTTEN JOB.
I JUS' GOT A SHOUT FROM VICTOR RAY.
WELL THEN GET YO' BIG LAZY ASS BACK IN BED, NIGGA, 'CAUSE YOU AIN'T GOT ONE-- NONE OF US DO.
GRAVES IS SITTIN' DOWN.
JESUS...
DID YOU BUST A NUT WHEN I...?

DAMMIT.
NERVOUS, TIBO?
I'M APPREHENSIVE.
ISN'T THAT THE SAME THING? BEHOLDER, BEHOLDEE?
NOT AT ALL. NERVES ARE IN THE EYES, AND FINGERS. APPREHENSION?...
"BACK OF THE NECK.
"WHEN YOU MISS THE EYES YOU DON'T HAVE."
WHY ISN'T AUGUSTUS HERE YET?
BECAUSE AUTHORITY ALWAYS NEEDS TO MAKE AN ENTRANCE.

YOU THINK HE'S STILL HOLDING THAT POSITION?
OF COURSE, CLINGING TO IT, NOW MORE THAN EVER.
"FOR ALL HIS NEW IDEAS, HE FINDS HIMSELF THE LAST OF THE OLD SCHOOL...
WHAT HE SUGGESTS, WE DON'T DISMISS. BUT IT'S OUR AGENDA WE AGREE TO, AND NOTHING LESS.
"WHAT IF HE DOESN'T?"
"DO YOU THINK AUGUSTUS IS A SMART MAN, TIBO?"
WELL, THAT MAKES HIM WHAT WE NEED HIM TO BE...

"...A SURVIVOR."
HEY.
HEY.
I SPOKE WITH CRETE.
SORRY I'M NOT A GOOD SHOT.
BENITO...
Y'KNOW, THAT WAS A STUPID THING TO DO.
YEAH, WELL...
YEAH.
MY HEART WAS IN THE RIGHT PLACE. THE BULLET, THOUGH?
LITTLE LOW.

"ANY IDEA WHERE THAT MAD MOTHER-FUCKER IS?"
"SAME PLACE HE'S ALWAYS BEEN..."
OUT THERE, DIZ.
HMM.
DON'T WORRY, THOUGH. CRETE HAS THIS PLACE ON LOCKDOWN.
YOU'RE SAFE.
HE GOT OUT. HE'LL GET BACK IN.
I PROMISE, BENITO...
...I WON'T LET LONO KILL YOU.
YOU WORKING FOR ME NOW?...

"...I'D BE CAREFUL ABOUT THAT."
I GOT THE FEELIN' WE BEEN FUCKIN' PLAYED. ALL ALONG, SINCE DAY ONE.
YOU MEAN ATLANTIC CITY.
"YEAH, BUT NO. I MEAN... LOOK, WHEN THE TRUST DECIDED THEY DIDN'T NEED US ANYMORE... AN' WHAT WE DID THEN IN A.C., WE THOUGHT THAT WAS THE START.
SANDMAN
MOTEL
TAXI
"THE BEGINNING OF THE END. BECAUSE THAT'S THE WAY IT WAS PRESENTED."
ACTUALLY, IT STARTED WHEN GRAVES TOLD THE TRUST NO TO THE EXPANSION JOB.
"NO, JACK, NOT THEN EITHER. WAS NO WAY GRAVES WOULD HAVE AGREED TO THE MINUTEMEN DOIN' WHAT THEY WERE ASKIN'--THE TRUST'S BORDERS WERE WRITTEN IN BLOOD, FROM SEA TO SHINING SEA."
1525

THEY KNEW THEY'D GET A NO.
THEY FUCKIN' KNEW IT--NOT ALL OF 'EM...BUT, THE ONES THAT DID...
WHAT I THINK IS THAT--STEALIN' ANOTHER COUNTRY WAS AN EXCUSE...
"FOR STEALIN' THIS ONE FROM THEMSELVES.
"AN' THEY USED THE MINUTEMEN TO DO IT.
"WE WERE PLAYED."
YOU THINK GRAVES WAS IN ON IT?

I DONE ENOUGH THINKIN', LOOP.
IT'S TIME TO KNOW.
WHAT DO YOU SAY, HIJACK?
BD-RING
VICTOR?
NOT 'LESS HE LOST HIS CELLIE ON THE WAY HERE. NUMBER'S LOCAL.
YO.
WAIT--YOU TOLD HIM WHERE--

?...
LOOPH?
LONO?
...SHUNNY DAYS.

JOHNSON
XIII

"WHATEVER HAPPENS TONIGHT...THIS MEETING, IT'S NOT GONNA GO WELL."
WHAT MAKES YOU THINK THAT?
CALL IT A HUNCH.
WHOSE?
MINE. AND THAT COUNTS FOR SOMETHING.
LOOK, THERE'S NOTHING TO GAIN-- NOBODY INVOLVED IS WALKING OUT A WINNER.
MAYBE THAT'S NOT THE POINT.
DIZZY...

TO WIN IS ALWAYS THE POINT.
BENITO!
MY FOOLISH BOY.
OH. SO YOU HEARD ABOUT LONO...
YES, SON...
I DID.

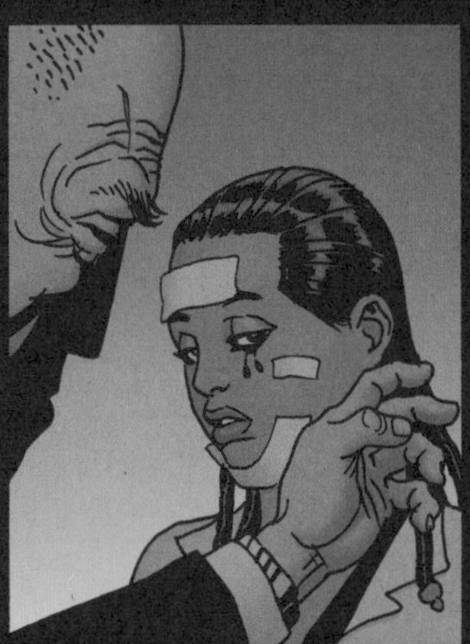

FORGIVE ME.

"100
BULLETS"

CHAPTER
ELEVEN
BOOTS ON

MY, MY, BOYS...
...WHAT KINDA SICK-FUCK PARTY DID I INTERRUPT?
CARE TO JOIN HER?
WORDS OUTTA MY MOUTH, COLE.
LOOPH? WHA' THE HELL IS GOIN' ON?

KEEP YER EYE ON THE PRIZE, LOOP--OR THE PRIZE WILL BLOW YER HEAD OFF.

DON' WORRY 'BOUT MY HEAD, COLE--WORRY ON' YER OWN...

SITTIN' DOWN.
WOULDN' DO THAT, I WERE YOU.
YER NOT ME.
LOOPH! GODDAMMA! WHA'THA FUGH?
LI'L BUSY HERE, LONO, SOME SCANDALOUS SHIT.
I DON' WANNA KILL YOU, VICTOR.
DON' WANNA KILL YOU NEITHER, LOOP...

TAKE SOME COMFORT IN THAT, IF I DO.
NOW, WAY I SEE IT?...
...THIS ENDS ONE OF TWO WAYS.
THREE.
?
THERE'S THREE WAYS.
HMM... INSIGHTFUL, JACKO.
NONO NONONO NO...
FUGH HIM--HE'S NEVAH RIGH-- THERE'S ONLY ONE WAY!
DO IT!
KILL EEJ OTHER-- IT'S WHA' THEY WAN' YA TO DO!

GEA THE FUGH OUTTA THE TRUST'S WAY! GIV'AH TO 'EM!
GIVE 'EM EVERYTHIN' THEY FUGHIN' WAN'!
I'S WHAT GRAVES WANS TOO--GEA THE FUGH OUTTA HIS WAY!
DO IT!
PULL THE FUGHIN' TRIGGERS YOU MUTHAFUGHIN' PUSSY SHITHEAD FAGGAH PUSSY FUGHIN' SONS A' BITCHES!
KILL EEJ OTHER AN' GET OUT OF MY FUCKIN' WAY!

NONE A' YOU MATTER NO MORE!
LEAS' OF ALL YOU, LI'L HUGHES!
I NEVER COULD FUCKIN' RELY ON YOU!
ALL THAT FUCKIN' TRAININ' AN' YOU DIN' LEARN DICK!
HEY, COLE...
BAA...

--AAAM
THANK YOU ALL FOR LETTING THIS MEETING HAPPEN HERE, IN MY HOUSE. IT SHOWS GREAT CHARACTER, WHEN NONE CERTAINLY WAS DESERVED.
XIII
THANK YOU, AUGUSTUS, FOR ACKNOWLEDGING.
AND FOR THE APOLOGY, AS IT WERE.
XIII
WHICH--BY THE WAY--IS ACCEPTED.
AND THANK YOU FOR THAT, MEGAN.
WHATEVER YOU MAY THINK, WHAT HAPPENED BETWEEN US PERSONALLY--
--IS NOT FOR THIS ROOM. OR OVER.
NO, IT HAS TO BE. FOR THE GOOD OF THE TRUST.
HA.

THE PAST IS THE PAST. IT'S TIME TO MOVE ON.
AH. I SEEM TO RECALL THE "THE FUTURE" SPEECH...
WELL THEN, TIBO...
...WHAT ARE THE TERMS OF MY SURRENDER?
AUGUSTUS, THAT'S NOT WHY WE'RE--
IT SHOULD BE.
ALL RIGHT. WE DECIDED-- FOR THE GOOD OF THE TRUST...
...THE HOUSE OF MEDICI STANDS, BUT YOU LOSE YOUR VOTE AT OUR TABLE.

WE WILL ACCEPT--AND VALUE--YOUR COUNSEL, BUT ULTIMATELY, YOU WON'T HAVE A SAY IN THE TRUST'S AFFAIRS.
THIS IS MY PUNISHMENT?
YES. YOURS.
WITH AMNESTY?
OF COURSE. WHICH BRINGS US TO...
THE MINUTEMEN.
TO MAKE THE TRUST HONEST ONCE MORE, THE MINUTEMEN ARE TO BE REINSTATED.
AGREED.
BUT UNDER A NEW AGENT.

OVER MY DEAD--
GRAVES PICKS HIS SUCCESSOR.
AUGUSTUS...HE CAN SUGGEST--
NO. AS LONG AS HIS CHOICE IS A CURRENT MINUTEMAN, IT'S HIS DECISION.
I'LL AGREE TO YOUR CONDITIONS, IF THIS IS AGREEABLE TO YOU.
IT IS.
THEN WE ARE DECIDED.
XIII

NOW YOUR FIRST ORDER OF BUSINESS, I IMAGINE, IS WHA BECOMES OF THE HOUSE OF VASCO.
JAVIER LEFT NO HEIRS, AND SLICING IT UP IS NO OPTION ANYMORE...
NOT AFTER WE JUST AGREED TO PUT OUR KNIVES AWAY.
I TAKE IT YOU HAVE A SUGGESTION?
PHIL, WOULD YOU EXCUSE US, PLEASE?...

"I GOTTA *TELL* YOU, KID..."

THAT WAS A *HELL* OF A THING TO DO.
PUT THAT FUCKIN' BULLET RIGHT WHERE IT *NEEDED* TO BE. WAS *WICKED*.
YEAH, WELL...

"...I LEARNED FROM THE *BEST*."
"YOU WAN' A *SAY* A FEW WORDS?"
"NAH. GOODBYE."

KINDA CRAZY, YOU WRAPPIN' THAT *PAINTING* AROUN' THE BODY. WASN'T IT *PRICELESS?*

ONLY TO THOSE THAT COULD *AFFORD* IT.

LIKE *ANY* PIECE A' ART, SAME STORY.
THE HONEY?
NOBODY. JUST A THIEF. WORKIN' THE TRUST-- MEGAN DIETRICH IN *PARTICULAR*. GOT IN OVER HER HEAD...
AN' IT ENDED UP ON THE *PAINTIN'*.

BOYS HERE BROUGHT ME UP TO *SPEED*...

"WE GOT A JOB NEEDS FINISHIN'."
HE ALWAYS LIKE THAT, DIZZY?
PRETTY MUCH, YEAH.
ONLY NOW, EVEN MORE.
THEY BEEN IN THERE, WHAT--THREE HOURS?
AT LEAST THE SHOUTING'S QUIETED DOWN. WHAT YOU THINK THAT WAS ABOUT?
NOTHING LESS THAN THE FATE OF THE WORLD, I'M SURE.
HEH.
HA HAHA HA--
PHIL?...
CAN YOU COME IN HERE, PLEASE?

WHY? TO COLLECT MY SEVERANCE PACKAGE?
SOMETHING LIKE THAT.
MR. GRAVES... PHIL...
GO TO HELL, MISS D'ARCY.
CARE TO JOIN ME?
IN LIGHT OF THE CIRCUMSTANCES SURROUNDING THE HOUSE OF VASCO...
...AND COMPELLING ARGUMENTS PUT FORTH BY OUR COUNSEL...
...THE TRUST HAS VOTED TO REASSIGN THE HOUSE, A SEAT AT OUR TABLE, AND THE RESPONSIBILITY TO ACT IN OUR BEST INTERESTS.
DO YOU ACCEPT?

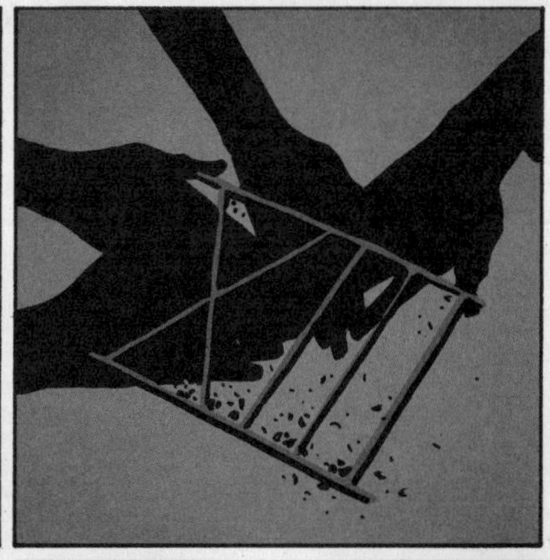

AUGUSTUS?

BENITO?...

WHAT ARE YOU DOING?

RESIGNING.
I ACCEPTED THE TRUST'S PUNISHMENT AS MINE, AND MINE ALONE. I CEDE ALL CONTROL OVER THE HOUSE OF MEDICI TO MY SON...

"...LONG LIVE THE NEW TRUST."
YOU PISSED AT ME?
FOR WHAT--TRUSTING MY REFLEXES? WAS SOME GENIUS SHIT, LOOP...
NOT LIKE IT WAS NO SUCKER PUNCH.
GOTTA SAY, VICTOR RAY, I'M SURPRISED. YOU AIN'T ONE TO QUESTION GRAVES.
YEAH, COLE, WELL, NEITHER WERE YOU.
THE FACT THAT NOW YOU ARE HOLDS SOME WATER WITH ME.
"SO, WHAT'S THE PLAN FER GETTIN' IN TO MEDICI'S, VIC?"
"WE'LL GO THROUGH THE FRONT GATE."

"REALLY? JUST ROLL ON UP, TELL 'EM WE GOT US UNFINISHED BUSINESS?"
"SOMETHING LIKE THAT."
WE'VE BEEN PLAYED FOR FOOLS!
YES, NOW CALM DOWN, SO YOU DON'T ACT ONE.
ACCEPT THE FACT. WE GOT PLAYED BY THE BEST.
AGAIN.
GRAVES HAD TO BE IN ON IT.
I DON'T THINK HE WAS.
WHAT? WE FUCKING GAVE A HOUSE TO THE MINUTEMEN!
WE GAVE A SEAT TO GRAVES. AND HE ACCEPTED, DESPITE HIS CONVICTIONS.
THAT WON'T SIT WITH THE MINUTEMEN.
WE WANTED THEM ON OUR SIDE-- WHICH NOW HAS GRAVES. AUGUSTUS'S MOVE...HE ANTICIPATED THIS. SO NOW...

"...IT'S OUR TURN."
BENITO...
MIND IF I JOIN YOU?
SHOULDN'T I BE ASKING YO
THAT QUESTION, MEGAN?
NO... I DON'T MIND.
...IF YOU'RE UP FOR IT.
YOU'D JUST LEAVE MY FATHER LIKE THAT, HUH?
YOUR FATHER AND I AREN'T. IT WAS HIS DECISION.
SEEMS HE MADE SOME BIG ONES TODAY.
CAN I MAKE ONE?
I NEED TO KNOW, BENITO, THAT YOU UNDERSTAND NOW, WE'RE IN THIS TOGETHER.

MEGAN... MY FATHER MADE SOME MISTAKES-- ONES I WON'T.
AND?
AND I DON'T THINK YOU--OR YOUR FRIENDS--
...FEEL THE SAME WAY.
BENITO... YOU DON'T KNOW HOW I FEEL...
BUT YOU'VE THOUGHT ABOUT IT, HAVEN'T YOU?
HAVEN'T YOU, MY BOY?

JOHNSON

"100 BULLETS"
FINALE:
A HOUSE OF GRAVES

WEATHER TWO, STATUS...
WEATHER TWO, COME IN...
WEATHER SIX?
SIR?
WEATHER TWO IS NOT RESPONDING.
I NEED YOU TO CHECK THEIR POSIT...

"WHAT IF IT'S NOT OPEN?
COLE, HE'S ON...
"WHAT IF LONO WAS SNOWIN' YOU AN' AIN'T ON BOARD?"
...A SERIOUS HATE.

MR. MEDICI... BENITO--
DROWNED?
YES, BUT STRANGLED. MURDER.
I'M SORRY.
...UNLESS THAT'S A CONFESSION, YOU'RE NOT RESPONSIBLE.
I WILL FIND WHO IS.
THAT'S NOT YOUR RESPONSIBILITY, EITHER.
IT'S DIZZY'S.
MISS CORDOVA, HERE, IS THE AGENT OF THE MINUTEMEN.

WHAT? YOU CAN'T BE SERIOUS, GRAVES!
TIBO...I SERIOUSLY CAN'T BE ANYTHING ELSE.
"YOU ALL AGREED THAT I WOULD NAME MY REPLACEMENT. NOW I HAVE.
"SHE'S BEEN TRAINED--BY ME, AND MR. SHEPHERD BEFORE ME. SHE'S QUALIFIED."
SHE'S--A SHE--NOT TO MENTION A SPI--
WE WILL REFER TO HER AS AGENT CORDOVA.
"I UNDERSTAND YOUR OBJECTIONS..."

...I JUST WON'T TOLERATE THEM.
BAMBAMBAMBAMBAMBA
PLEASE GET IN THE HOUSE.
YOU WANT TO TELL ME--
--TO DO YOUR JOB?
FINE. DO IT.
YOU HAVE CARTE BLANCHE-- AGAIN.
BENITO WAS MURDERED. HE WAS A HEAD OF HOUSE.
SETTLE THE BILL.

GET THE GATE.

WAIT--

THESE ARE OUR...

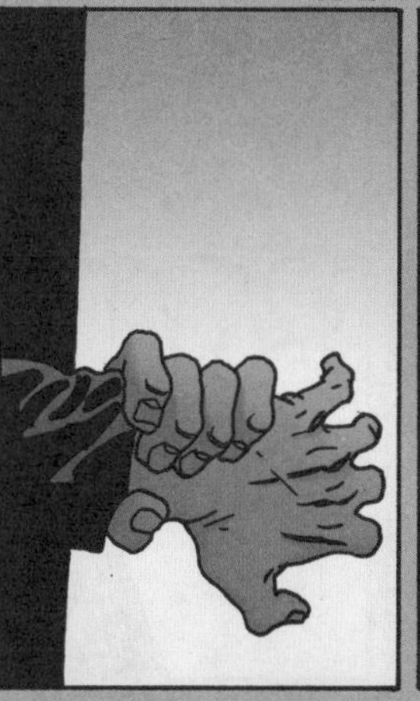

BAM

...I THOUGHT YOU WERE RETIRED, DAD.
I AM, VICTOR RAY...
WORK FOR MYSELF NOW. MONEY WAS GOOD SO I TOOK THIS JOB, BUT NOW?
I'M LEAVIN' IT.
TOO MANY GRINDIN' AXES FOR ME.
YOU MIGHT THINK ABOUT PUTTIN' YERS DOWN.
YOU SHOULD GO.
WELL, THAT'S WHAT I WAS FITTIN' TO DO, SO...
OKAY.
MY FLIGHT BACK TO CHICAGO AIN'T UNTIL TOMORROW, THOUGH...
TOMORROW? SHIT, OLD MAN...

"THAT'S ALREADY TODAY."
YOU SHOULD RECONSIDER...
WHAT? WHY? MEGAN, YOU'VE ALREADY TALKED ME INTO MAKING ONE MISTAKE, SO SAVE YOUR BREATH ON ANOTHER.
THIS WAS FOOLISH-COMING HERE I'VE BEEN SET UP!
YOU?
WE--NO--YES, ME. AND DON'T PLAY THE DUMB BLONDE, OKAY?
JOAN... ROTHSTEIN...
THAT WAS YOUR MISTAKE.
BULLSHIT...I NEVER THOUGHT LEAVING GRAVES TO HIS OWN DEVICES WAS SMART.
THE REST OF YOU... AS LONG AS GRAVES HAD HIS GAME...
I CAN'T BELIEVE I WAS SO STUPID TO BE PART OF GIVING HIM A HOUSE!

YOU DON'T SEE IT, DO YOU? THAT YOUR "STUPIDITY" IS THE ONE THING THAT CAN SAVE YOU...
NO.
NO, MEGAN, I DON'T.
TIBO? I'M...

WHY DID YOU TRY TO KILL ME?
I--HUH? AREN'T?--
I WAS DOING MY JOB.
CRAACK

MR. DAW.
THAT MAKES TWO OF US.
I'M SURPRISED THAT YOU'RE STILL ALIVE.
...SHOULD GET OUT OF MY WAY, CRETE.
NO SIR, I SHOULDN'T.
"GRAVES--THE MINUTEMEN ARE IN!"
"OF COURSE THEY ARE."

...THEY HAVE A JOB TO FINISH.
SMACK
CALL THEM OFF!
I DID.
YOU'RE FULL OF SHIT...
SMAACK
TIBO'S DEAD.
--ARE YOU...?
SO IS BENITO.

YES, MEGAN, I AM.
YOU MURDERED MY FATHER.
HE WAS MY FRIEND.
I HAD RESPECT FOR HIM.
SPI-TOO
SHIT IS THE BUSINESS WE'RE IN, MEGAN...
WHETHER WE'RE FULL
IT, OR DIGGING
OURSELVES
FROM UNDER
PILE OF IT...

SHIT HAPPENS.
AUGUSTUS... WE SHOULD HAVE A FEW WORDS.
I DON'T KNOW WHETHER TO COMMEND...

...UNTIL I SAW YOUR SON FLOATING DEAD IN THE POOL.
THAT WAS SOME THINKING ON YOUR FEET.

"I MEAN, BEING STRIPPED OF YOUR POWER...IT MUST HAVE BEEN QUITE A BLOW.
"AND THEN SELLING THE IDEA FOR ME TO TAKE OVER A HOUSE...TO MAKE THAT MAKE SENSE--NOT TO THE TRUST, MIND YOU--
BUT TO ME?
KUDOS.
"THEN CEDING CONTROL OVER THE HOUSE OF MEDICI TO BENITO--AFTER YOU KNEW HE HAD DESIGNS ON IT...
"BRILLIANT."

"YOU LEFT THE OTHER HOUSES NO CHOICE BUT TO KILL HIM TO MAINTAIN THE POWER STRUCTURE THEY CAME HERE DEMANDING.
"I'M FAIRLY CERTAIN THAT ALL THREE WERE INVOLVED. D'ARCY, VERMEER, AND DIETRICH ALL CONSPIRED AGAINST MEDICI...
MEANING ALL THREE WILL HAVE TO BE PUNISHED IN KIND.
THREE HOUSES, WITH NO HEIRS.
"LEAVING JUST TWO--YOURS AND MINE.
AND WITH ME LEFT TO CHOOSE OUR NEW AGENT, I'M SURE YOU THOUGHT THE THREAT OF THE MINUTEMEN WOULD BE NEUTRALIZED.

"SO HERE WE ARE, WITH THE FORMER MINUTEMEN STORMING THE GATES. DO YOU STILL BELIEVE I CAN CONTROL THEM?"
FUCK NO I DON'T.
DO YOU BELIEVE IN GOD?
NO.

BDAM
BLAMM
BDAHMM

...
THANK--
--DON'T.
I KNOW, DIZZY. WHAT YOU JUST DID...
KILLING SOMEONE SIMPLY FOR THE REASON YOU WANT THEM DEAD...

IT'S DIFFICULT-- FOR A MORAL PERSON.
WHAT'S RIGHT, AND WHAT'S WRONG...TO DECIDE IT?
THAT'S A FUCKING...BIG RESPONSIBILITY.
BUT IT'S DONE. SOMEONE'S DEAD. LIVE WITH IT.
MYSELF-- WHEN I'VE STRUGGLED... I'VE TAKEN COMFORT BELIEVING--
--SOME PEOPLE JUST DESERVE TO DIE?
YES. SOME DO.
YOU CONVINCED ME OF THAT.

"REALLY? I REMEMBER IT *DIFFERENTLY.*"

MISS DIETRICH?

WHAT ARE YOU DOING?
MY JOB.

RIGHT NOW...AGENT CORDOVA... YOUR *JOB* IS TO KEEP THE *TRUST* ALIVE.
PLEASE DON'T TELL ME WHAT MY JOB IS.

I HAVE A QUESTION...

DID YOU *LOVE* BENITO?

THAT'S NONE OF YOUR BUSINESS.

THAT SOUNDS LIKE A YES.

I DON'T BELIEVE YOU.

BENITO WAS...HE HAD A SPECIAL PLACE IN MY HEART.
MINE TOO.
THAT'S... CHARMING. VYING FOR THE LOVE OF A *DEAD MAN*.
HOW CAN YOU *SATISFY* IT?
EASY ANSWER
REVENGE.
"REVENGE? THAT'S FUNNY. SURE. IT *TOUCHES* YOU..."
BUT T'S NOT E *TOUCH* HAT YOU *MISS.*
WHAT'S THAT SM...?
DEAR GOD...

NO!
TRY HELL YES, MEGAN...
HELL YES.
DIZZY, YOU MIND?...
GASOLINE
GASOLINE
PLEASE...
HUH. WELL, I AM SURPRISED. I MEAN, I FIGURED A GIRL LIKE YOU...
"FOLLOWIN' IN HER OLD MAN'S FOOTSTEPS..."

"...SHE'D LIKE TO FINISH WHAT SHE STARTED."
LOOP...
YO, VIC.
HOOK THIS TO THE COIL WIRE FOR ME.
WHAT YOU DOIN'?
DONE, SON. I'M DONE.
JUST WASTED A CADRE A' MUTHAFUCKAS. DON' KNOW WHY, AN' WORSE? DON' FEEL NOTHIN' ABOUT IT...FUCKED SHIT.
I DON' WANNA BE LIKE YOU, VIC. SORRY.
FROOM
YER FATHER WOULD BE PROUD.
OF WHAT?
"LET ME TELL YOU WHAT I REMEMBER..."

...I REMEMBER DRUNKENLY WATCHING THE SUN COME UP, WHEN THE IDEA OF PUTTING THE TRUST'S POWER--IN AN ATTACHÉ--MADE SENSE...
I REMEMBER A BRAVE NEW WORLD. I REMEMBER A TRADE-OFF...MAKING A DEAL WITH...
I REMEMBER THAT TOO, AUGUSTUS...
"...IT'S ALWAYS THE DEVIL YOU KNOW, ISN'T IT?"
I THOUGHT YOU'D LIKE THIS...THAT YOUR END WOULD BE... WHAT'S THAT FRENCH WORD?
...MERDE?
NO. SHIT, NO--
APROPOS...
THAT'S THE ONE.
IT FITS.

LIKE A PAIR OF SHOES.
NICE ONES. EXPENSIVE ONES. THE KIND WORTH THE BLISTERS IT TAKES TO BREAK THEM IN.
OR IS IT THE OTHER WAY AROUND?...
DO THE SHOES BREAK US IN? I'VE BEEN PONDERIN' THAT...
WHAT'S YER TAKE, MEGAN?
HMM. NO USE TRYIN' TO PUT SOMETHIN' OUT I AIN'T STARTED YET...
CLIC

YOU KILLED YOUR SON.
NO. I LEFT THAT UP TO OTHERS.
YOU GAVE THEM NO CHOICE.
PLEASE... YOU OF ALL PEOPLE, GRAVES...
THE CHOICE IS ALWAYS THERE.

BAAM
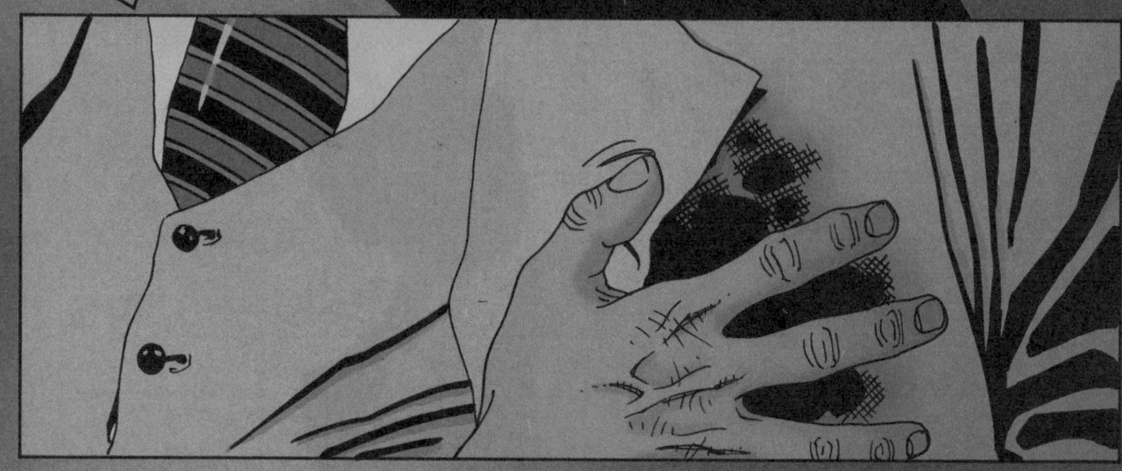

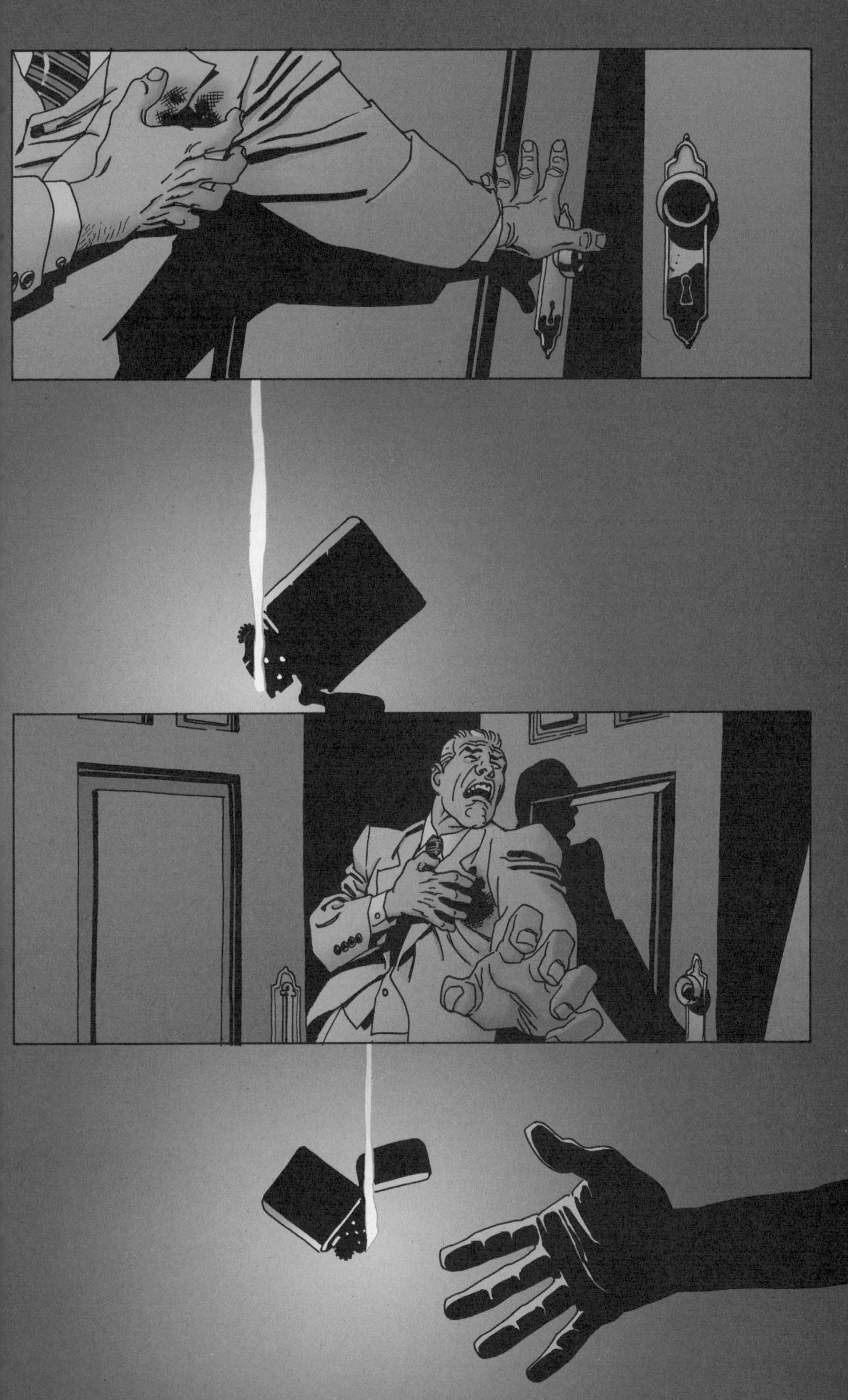

BOOOOOM

DIZZY!!
HANG ON, GIRL! HANG--
I CAN'T FEEL...
SHHH.
I DON'T FEEL...

MR. MEDICI...YOU KILLED HIM.
SHHH
YOU MADE A MOVE... MR. GRAVES, AGAINST ANOTHER HOUSE IN THE TRUST...
YES.
YES, AGENT CORDOVA, I DID.
YEARS AGO, HE RUINED MY LIFE--COMPROMISED MY PRINCIPLES--IN EXCHANGE FOR...
...GIVING ME THE OPPORTUNITY TO OFFER MY PRINCIPLES TO OTHER PEOPLE.
THEN... HE DIDN'T RUIN YOUR LIFE.

I KNOW.
THE END